MW01026838

*Set design by Marjorie Bradley Kellogg*          *Photo by Susan Johann*

A scene from the Signature Theatre Company
production of *Thief River*.

# THIEF RIVER

## BY LEE BLESSING

DRAMATISTS
PLAY SERVICE
INC.

THIEF RIVER
Copyright © 2002, Lee Blessing

All Rights Reserved

CAUTION: Professionals and amateurs are hereby warned that performance of THIEF RIVER is subject to payment of a royalty. It is fully protected under the copyright laws of the United States of America, and of all countries covered by the International Copyright Union (including the Dominion of Canada and the rest of the British Commonwealth), and of all countries covered by the Pan-American Copyright Convention, the Universal Copyright Convention, the Berne Convention, and of all countries with which the United States has reciprocal copyright relations. All rights, including professional/amateur stage rights, motion picture, recitation, lecturing, public reading, radio broadcasting, television, video or sound recording, all other forms of mechanical or electronic reproduction, such as CD-ROM, CD-I, DVD, information storage and retrieval systems and photocopying, and the rights of translation into foreign languages, are strictly reserved. Particular emphasis is placed upon the matter of readings, permission for which must be secured from the Author's agent in writing.

The stage performance rights in THIEF RIVER (other than first class rights) are controlled exclusively by DRAMATISTS PLAY SERVICE, INC., 440 Park Avenue South, New York, NY 10016. No professional or nonprofessional performance of the Play (excluding first class professional performance) may be given without obtaining in advance the written permission of DRAMATISTS PLAY SERVICE, INC., and paying the requisite fee.

Inquiries concerning all other rights should be addressed to Berman, Boals and Flynn, Inc., 208 West 30th Street, Suite 401, New York, NY 10001. Attn: Judy Boals.

**SPECIAL NOTE**

Anyone receiving permission to produce THIEF RIVER is required to give credit to the Author as sole and exclusive Author of the Play on the title page of all programs distributed in connection with performances of the Play and in all instances in which the title of the Play appears for purposes of advertising, publicizing or otherwise exploiting the Play and/or a production thereof. The name of the Author must appear on a separate line, in which no other name appears, immediately beneath the title and in size of type equal to 50% of the size of the largest, most prominent letter used for the title of the Play. No person, firm or entity may receive credit larger or more prominent than that accorded the Author. The following acknowledgment must appear on the title page in all programs distributed in connection with performances of the Play:

World premiere originally produced by
Signature Theatre Company, New York City
James Houghton, Founding Artistic Director
Bruce E. Whitacre, Managing Director

*Thief River* was supported by a playwright's residency
and public staged readings at the 2000 O'Neill Playwrights Conference
of the Eugene O'Neill Theater Center, Waterford, CT.

*To Jim Houghton and the Signature Theatre*

THIEF RIVER was presented as a staged reading at the Eugene O'Neill National Playwrights Conference in Waterford, Connecticut, on July 22, 2000. It was directed by Michael Engler; the set design was by G.W. Mercier; the lighting design was by Jane Cox; the sound design was by Robert Kaplowitz; the dramaturg was Kim Euell; the production stage manager was Catherine Bloch; and the production assistant was Katherine Lee Boyer. The cast was as follows:

GIL 1/JODY ........................................................ Dallas Roberts
RAY 1/ KIT ....................................................... Glenn Howerton
GIL 2/HARLOW ................................................... Sam Gregory
RAY 2/REESE ........................................................ Roscoe Born
GIL 3/PERRY .......................................................... Brian Smiar
RAY 3/ANSON ................................................... Mason Adams


THIEF RIVER was produced by the Signature Theatre Company (James Houghton, Founding Artistic Director; Bruce E. Whitacre, Managing Director) in New York City on May 20, 2001. It was directed by Mark Lamos; the set design was by Marjorie Bradley Kellogg; the lighting design was by Pat Collins; the music and sound design were by John Gromada; the costume design was by Jess Goldstein; the fight direction was by B.H. Barry; and the production stage manager was Michael McGoff. The cast was as follows:

GIL 1/JODY ........................................................ Jeffrey Carlson
RAY 1/ KIT ........................................................... Erik Sorensen
GIL 2/HARLOW ...................................................... Neil Maffin
RAY 2/REESE ................................................... Gregg Edelman
GIL 3/PERRY ................................................... Remak Ramsay
RAY 3/ANSON ................................................... Frank Converse

# CHARACTERS

GIL — 18

RAY — 18, his friend

HARLOW — mid-40s, a drifter

ANSON — late 60s, a farmer, Ray's grandfather

KIT — 21, an acquaintance of Gil

PERRY — 60s, Ray's father-in-law, a farmer

JODY — 17, Ray's grandson

REESE — 40, Harlow's nephew


# PLACE

The action in all three periods takes place in the empty living room of an abandoned farm house in the Midwest.


# TIME

June of three different years: 1948, 1973, 2001.


# CASTING NOTE

The play requires a cast of six, who double the roles as follows:

ACTOR A ... plays GIL at 18 *(GIL 1)* and JODY
ACTOR B ... plays RAY at 18 *(RAY 1)* and KIT
ACTOR C ... plays GIL at 43 *(GIL 2)* and HARLOW
ACTOR D ... plays RAY at 43 *(RAY 2)* and REESE
ACTOR E ... plays GIL at 73 *(GIL 3)* and PERRY
ACTOR F ... plays RAY at 73 *(RAY 3)* and ANSON

# THIEF RIVER

## ACT ONE

### Scene 1

*1948. Living room of an abandoned farmhouse. An arch-way leads to the front hall, another to the back of the house. First light of dawn on a June morning. Sound of sparrows in a tree outside builds to a surprising intensity, then stops amid a storm of wingbeats. Ray's voice can be heard at a distance from the house*

RAY. *(From outside.)* Gil! Gil!! Goddammit — ! *Gil* — !! *(Sound of the front door being forced open. A screen door slams. The eighteen-year-old Gil rushes in, sweaty. He's been running a long way. He wears a white early-fifties prom tux, which is torn, wet, covered with mud. His face is bruised. Dried blood as well. He stops in the middle of the room and starts to strip out of the tux.)*
GIL. Fuck!! Fuck, fuck, *fuck!! FUCK ME!* Just *fucking fuck me* — !!! *(He throws his jacket onto the couch, tears open his shirt, scattering studs on the floor, then starts pulling down his pants and falls in the process. He continues struggling to get them off — even though his shoes are still on — as Ray enters. Ray, in everyday clothes, has been chasing Gil awhile.)*
RAY. Gil — ! What are you *doing?!*
GIL. Look at me! Look at my tux — !
RAY. What in hell — ?!
GIL. I'm never gonna get my deposit back.
RAY. Why'd you run away out there?

GIL. I didn't know it was you. I thought it was Lewis.

RAY. *(As Gil struggles with the pants.)* What happened to you?

GIL. What do you think happened? *(Able to get only one pant leg over a shoe, giving up and sobbing.)* He pissed on me! He beat the shit out of me, and he pissed all over —

RAY. Didn't anybody help?

GIL. Who's gonna help me?!

RAY. The teachers —

GIL. They were all inside. He caught me in the fucking parking lot.

RAY. Don't talk like that —

GIL. How'm I supposed to talk? *Where were you?!*

RAY. You knew I wasn't coming to prom.

GIL. I don't care! You should've been there!

RAY. I'm sorry. I've been driving around all night, looking for you. Harriet Cochrane called me —

GIL. Harriet?! God! So *everybody* knows — !

RAY. She said Lewis beat you up. She didn't say you got pissed on.

GIL. That was later. I found him again.

RAY. Found — ? You went looking for him?!

GIL. What else was I gonna do?

RAY. Gil, what were you carrying?

GIL. What?

RAY. When you were on the road. You had something in your hand.

GIL. You got any clothes? I'm freezing.

RAY. It was a gun, right? You had a gun. *(Gil is silent.)* Where is it?

GIL. Out in the field. I threw it away.

RAY. Whose gun is it? Your Dad's? *(As Gil nods.)* Jesus. Hold on. I've got some clothes in the truck. *(Starting out, then hesitating.)* We gotta clean you off. I don't think there's any water here — wait a minute. *(Ray hurries out. Gil starts on his shoe once more, finally wrestling it off without untying it. He does the same with the other shoe and gets his pants off. He's down to his boxer shorts by now. He sits shivering next to the heap of reeking clothes. A muffled smash out on the porch and Ray reenters with muddy overalls and a bottle of tonic water. The top's been broken off.)* Anson went to the liquor store today. He told me to bring it all in, but I forgot a box. Lucky, huh?

GIL. You gonna wash me in gin?

RAY. It's tonic. Come on. You really stink.

GIL. Thanks.

RAY. Careful — it's broken glass.

GIL. Cut my throat — what do I care?

RAY. Stop it. *(Gingerly, Ray pours water over Gil's head. He rubs him down with his free hand.)*

GIL. It's cold!

RAY. Get everywhere he peed on you, okay? *(As Gil washes himself in this makeshift shower, Ray pulls off his own jacket and offers it.)* Here — dry off. *(As Gil hesitates, rubbing him with the jacket.)* Do it! *(Gil takes over drying himself. Ray points at the wet clothes.)* We'll get the gun, throw this stuff in the truck, and take you home.

GIL. I'm not going home!

RAY. Why'd you have your Dad's gun?

GIL. Why do you think? I was gonna kill Lewis.

RAY. Kill — !? What are you saying? You took it to the dance?

GIL. *After* the dance. When he beat me up the first time. That's when I went and got it.

RAY. What in hell's wrong with you?

GIL. All I wanted to do was go to my own prom. Just be there. Just look good and … you know, watch people.

RAY. Watch Lewis, you mean.

GIL. He's beautiful.

RAY. You can't say that.

GIL. But he can piss all over me? Great — I'll remember.

RAY. We talked about this, Gil. You're special. You can't help it. You're a special way and you can't expect to — *(Gil suddenly kisses Ray, hard on the mouth. Ray is startled, but doesn't push him away at first. Ray finally pushes Gil away and wipes his mouth angrily.)* We promised we'd never do that again — !!

GIL. I never thought I'd get pissed on, either.

RAY. How do you expect me to be your friend?

GIL. You are my friend. *(Ray stares at him a moment, then turns away. Without looking at Gil, Ray holds out the jacket and overalls.)*

RAY. Shut up. Get these on.

GIL. *(Dressing.)* Want to know what Lewis called me, after he beat me up in the parking lot?

RAY. Not especially.

GIL. I been collecting 'em — the names he calls me. There's faggot and fruit and fairy — don't know why they all start with "f." Or maybe I do.

RAY. Stop it.

GIL. Tonight, though. You know what he called me? Standing there with the other kids around us, watching me trying to catch my blood in my hands? "Fragile." *(Laughs.)* "That's what you get, you little fragile." He made it a noun, the stupid —

RAY. Gil —

GIL. I kinda liked it. Gonna get a dog and name him that.

RAY. Nobody's up yet. Maybe we can slip you in without —

GIL. I'm not going home.

RAY. What are you talking about?

GIL. You don't know what I did. You have no idea what I did.

RAY. You got beat up.

GIL. No, after. I fired the gun, Ray. I shot him.

RAY. Who?

GIL. Lewis! I found him parked. About an hour ago. He was naked in the back seat with — I don't know, some girl. I couldn't see her. They didn't know I was there. The window was partly down. I could hear 'em. I pointed the gun at him — stuck it right in the window.

RAY. Oh God, Gil —

GIL. I couldn't, though. Couldn't shoot. He was so beautiful. How could I hurt him? How could I hurt something as beautiful as that?

RAY. But you said —

GIL. The girl screamed. Opened her eyes and saw me or something, I don't know. I must've looked scary as hell. Had all this caked blood on my face and shit like that —

RAY. Watch your language. What did he do?

GIL. He smiled. He just smiled, said, "Hi, Gil — back for more?" and got out. He didn't even cover up. He stood there naked, smiling at me. He was still, you know, hard. *(Almost smiling.)* Wasn't for me. Wasn't even for that girl. It was 'cause he knew how bad he was gonna hurt me. He walked up, took the gun away and dropped it on the ground. Then he slugged me. Right here. I don't even remember hitting the ground. Then he got down on one knee and started slugging me again — hard as he could, over and over, till I passed out. When I woke up, he was pissing on me. His girl was telling him to quit it, but he wouldn't. He finished up, handed me back my gun, said "Drop by anytime," and got back in his car — in the backseat. He was going back to what he was doing, you know? He didn't even shut the door.

RAY. Is that when you shot him?

GIL. I couldn't see good. I was still on the ground. I aimed the gun at him, right at his white, perfect … bouncing ass. Follow the bouncing ball, right? And I pulled the trigger.

RAY. Did you hit him?

GIL. No, I hit the front tire. He yelled and hauled out of the car again and came at me. So I shot again. I was just trying to make him stop. I was aiming for the back tire. But he screamed. He fell. I think I hit him in the hand. He was holding his hand and rolling around. I think I got some fingers. That's when I ran. I just kept running.

RAY. My God, Gil —

GIL. I ran all the way over to Marchetti's Pure Oil, over on the highway, and hid behind there. When it started getting light, I thought this'd be better. If anybody came here, it'd be you. *(Suddenly panicky.)* What are they gonna do? What are they gonna do to me, Ray?

RAY. Nothing. You're going to be all right.

GIL. I don't know why I got that gun. I've never been like that. I didn't know I could get like that.

RAY. It wasn't your fault.

GIL. It was. But I don't care anymore. Hug me, Ray?

RAY. What?

GIL. Nothing else, just hug me. *(Ray hesitates, then hugs Gil. They sit on the floor in each other's arms.)* You sneaked out, right? Anson doesn't know you're here?

RAY. He was sleeping. *(Harlow, in torn and filthy clothes, suddenly appears in the archway that leads to the back of the house.)*

HARLOW. So was I. *(Startled, the two boys jump up. Though Harlow looks shaggy and beaten down, he's powerfully built and dangerous-looking. He pulls out a straight razor and opens it with a practiced motion.)* My name's Harlow. Where's that gun? *(Gil suddenly bolts for the archway leading to the front door.)*

RAY. Gil — !! *(Harlow intercepts him and hurls him to the floor. In an instant Harlow's on top of the struggling Gil, razor to his throat.)*

11

HARLOW. You got a sunny disposition? Huh, boy? Huh?

RAY. Don't hurt him — !

HARLOW. You find that gun — right now — or I'm gonna carve a smile in this little faggot's face he ain't ever gonna lose. *(The three of them freeze. Lights shift subtly. The fortyish Ray 2 enters. He moves around the room, taking it all in. He nods at Harlow.)*

RAY 2. *(To audience.)* That's Harlow. This is the only time we ever met. *(Pointing at the young Ray.)* That's me. I looked okay then, didn't I? Not exactly Lewis, maybe, but ... okay. *(As he continues Ray, Gil and Harlow all slowly exit by turn.)* This house is on my farm. My Dad built it, right after he got back from World War Two. I remember, we worked on the house all summer — my Dad, my grandfather Anson, and me. Dad never stopped; he wouldn't even take breaks. He was a lot more nervous than before. He'd done things in the war, you could tell. Things he couldn't talk about. He worked on the house like he was afraid it wouldn't get done. When it finally was finished, he seemed to take this strange kind of breath. *(A beat.)* A week before we moved in, he shot my mother. Then he shot himself. If I'd been home, he would've shot me. Battle fatigue. They buried him with full honors. Town couldn't do enough for me after that. Anson finished raising me. Nobody ever lived in this house. *(Ray 2 exits the way he came. Lights shift again: Ray reenters in spotlight. When Ray speaks, it's not to address the audience directly. These are bits of letters he's written.)*

RAY. I'm glad you're out of danger, Gil. Anson won't let me come see you. Won't even let me call. Anyhow, I know you like my handwriting. I'll try to make it better'n usual. Hope you're not in pain. The doctor says there'll be a scar, but maybe not too big. I dreamed about you last night. Like most nights. It's better than not seeing you at all. You were naked. Like most nights. I don't mean to dream about you like that. Just happens. *(A beat.)* You're gonna get well. I know it. You'll be like new — except, you know, the scar. Anson won't even let me off the farm right now. Said he's afraid I'll run into somebody else like Harlow. *(After a beat.)* You were so beautiful in my dream. Naked. Like that time you said the river was too cold. *(Ray exits. Action continues without pause as lights crossfade into:)*

# Scene 2

*1973. Late afternoon on a bright, sunny day. The fortyish Gil 2 enters. He wears an off-the-rack sportscoat and slacks — the effect is midwestern. He has a scar running down the side of his neck from just below his ear to his throat. With him is Perry, a man in his sixties. Perry's in casual clothes. He seems upset and confused about something.*

PERRY. I never in my life seen Ray as mad as that. He's the coolest head in town — ask anybody around here. That was a wedding rehearsal, for God's sake. What in hell were you doing there?

GIL 2. Seeing an old friend.

PERRY. Friend?! Hell of a way to do that.

GIL 2. I didn't know they were having the rehearsal today.

PERRY. You could've phoned first. *(As the floor suddenly squeaks ominously under Gil 2's foot.)* Careful where you step.

GIL 2. I'm surprised this place hasn't fallen down.

PERRY. Ray keeps it up, sorta. Won't let anybody live in it. Won't sell it, either. *(As Gil 2 nods.)* He's always out here, patching things up. All day, sometimes. Molly gets mad. I keep out of it.

GIL 2. Why'd we come out here?

PERRY. How the hell should I know? It's where Ray said. He'll be here in a minute. Had to cool down Ray Junior. Ray Junior would've killed that little — What the hell's wrong with that kid of yours, anyway?

GIL 2. *(Meditatively.)* Ray Junior.

PERRY. Yeah — his son. Why's your kid still outside?

GIL 2. Father of the groom. Ray's the father of ... *(Fascinated by the word.)* Father. *(Perry looks out a window.)*

PERRY. He's just wandering around out there, out in the field. Didn't he ever see a farm before? Who are you people, anyhow?

GIL 2. You don't recognize me?

PERRY. Am I supposed to?

GIL 2. I'll give you a hint. *(Displaying his scar.)* This look familiar? *(As Perry shrugs.)* Gil. My name's Gil. Ray's friend, back in high school? I shot a kid named Lewis? I left town? *(Perry stares at him.)*
PERRY. I thought you died. *(A beat.)*
GIL 2. You're Ray's father-in-law?
PERRY. That's right. Perry. Molly's dad. *(Gil 2 extends his hand. Perry hesitates, then shakes his hand.)*
GIL 2. So — what's your daughter like these days?
PERRY. Fine before you showed up. Don't know what kind of trouble you brought for her and Ray, but —
GIL 2. What's between me and Ray is our business.
PERRY. All I know is, Ray's the most respected man in this town. Nobody works harder, nobody farms better, nobody cares about people more'n he does. His son's about to marry a beautiful girl. Ray's built up a whole life out of the worst tragedy a kid could have. I don't know what decent man would want to trouble that. *(Turning to the window again.)* That boy of yours is a piece of work. He insane or what?
GIL 2. I want to apologize for him —
PERRY. Apologize? He walks in the middle of the wedding rehearsal, singing "Here Comes The Bride" at the top of his lungs —
GIL 2. I tried to stop him —
PERRY. Marches up the aisle, grabs Ray Junior's fiancee, kisses her in front of the minister and everybody — and you want to apologize? I've never seen anything like it. If we hadn't dived in, Ray Junior would've turned that boy of yours into compost. Got a couple good shots in as it was. He got you too, didn't he? That hurt much?
GIL 2. *(Touching his jaw tenderly.)* Yeah.
PERRY. Good. Where in hell you living now?
GIL 2. Brooklyn Center.
PERRY. Down in the cities? Long trip.
GIL 2. Five hours. *(Another pause. Perry looks out the window again.)*
PERRY. Your boy's coming this way. How old did you say he was?
GIL 2. He's twenty-one. And he's not my son.
PERRY. Sorry. Nephew?
GIL 2. Friend.
PERRY. Kinda young for a friend.
GIL 2. Actually, he's just about the right age. We sleep together.

14

PERRY. Oh? *Oh.* Okay, you mean…?

GIL 2. We have sexual relations on a more or less regular basis.

PERRY. Okay.

GIL 2. If that makes you uncomfortable —

PERRY. *(Uncomfortably.)* No, no. I don't mind. I've met, um …

GIL 2. Gay?

PERRY. People, yeah. I've met 'em.

GIL 2. I thought you knew I was gay. When I lived here. Thought everyone knew.

PERRY. We just knew you were different, that's all. Tried not to think about it. 'Sides, you were a kid. Folks thought you should have a chance to, I don't know …

GIL 2. Grow out of it?

PERRY. Yeah.

GIL 2. You sure it's not a problem?

PERRY. 'Course not. I'm tolerant. I watch TV. You're marching now, you've got bands, glee clubs. You're on Cronkite every damn night — *(Kit walks in, looking irritable. Unlike Gil, Kit's outfit makes no concessions to country tastes. His look is fashionable and cheap. It does not scream seventies — he's more sophisticated than that. But his clothes are tight and seductive. They make Perry uneasy.)*

KIT. It's a *farm.*

GIL 2. Kit — there you are. I was just telling Perry here about you and me. It seems he's tolerant.

KIT. He is?

GIL 2. That's what he says.

KIT. Good. 'Cause I have been dying to suck your cock. *(To Perry.)* Can you wait in the car for ten minutes?

GIL 2. *(Angrily.)* Stop that! Right now! This bullshit is not going to work, Kit. You understand? It will not work. *(To Perry.)* I'm sorry.

PERRY. *(Keeping his distance.)* That's all right.

KIT. It's a *farm.*

GIL 2. So what!?

KIT. You said just the town. You said we didn't have to go near a farm.

GIL 2. It's farm country! There are going to be farms!

KIT. I'm *nervous.*

GIL 2. This act is not going to get you anything you want — is

15

that clear? Now go outside. Throw rocks at something.

KIT. Let me alone — ! I've been beat up! *(With a huge sigh of exasperation, dumping himself on the floor, face down.)* I'm gonna climb this floor.

GIL 2. Goddammit, Kit —

KIT. Can you climb a floor, Gil? I'm gonna climb it from one end to the other. *(Kit starts crawling along the floor, "climbing" it with exaggerated effort. They watch him for a moment.)*

PERRY. That boy has problems.

KIT. I can't believe you brought me to a farm. Where am I from, Gil?

GIL 2. No one cares where you're from.

KIT. I'm from Appleton, Wisconsin. Appleton! Wisconsin! I grew up on farms. Until I was fifteen, I was covered in cow manure. Cows used to shit on me.

GIL 2. Kit —

KIT. We were poor. So poor we had to *eat* cow manure. For us, cow pies were really pies.

GIL 2. Will you shut up?

KIT. *Why did you bring me here?!* *(To Perry.)* You know who was from Appleton, don't you? Senator Joseph R. McCarthy.

GIL 2. He wasn't gay people — he was communists.

KIT. Yeah, and who were the worst communists? The *gay* communists!

GIL 2. *(Trying to pull Kit up.)* Will you stop this?!

KIT. Can I please suck your cock?

GIL 2. That's it. *(Gil 2 grabs Kit and pulls him up.)*

KIT. Hey — !

GIL 2. Get outside and stay there! *(Gil 2 runs Kit out of the room, flinging him outside. We hear Kit shout from off.)*

KIT. *(Off.)* I'm not coming back in!

GIL 2. Good!! *(Returning, to Perry.)* I'm sorry. Gay man in a rural setting. Kit and I don't usually fight like this.

PERRY. This some kind of special occasion? *(From far off outside we hear Kit.)*

KIT. *(Off.)* It's a *farm!*

PERRY. Your little friend's lucky it's me he's behaving like that around. Plenty of men in this town would love to take a guy like him apart.

GIL 2. I grew up here, remember?

PERRY. So? You should've known better. *(Another silence.)* What kind of work you do?

GIL 2. Travel writer.

PERRY. Yeah? My wife and I stay at inns. *(A beat.)*

GIL 2. You farm?

PERRY. Used to. Got out. Economics.

GIL 2. Right.

PERRY. My best friend got out, too. Last year. Foreclosure.

GIL 2. What's he do now?

PERRY. He blew his head off with a shotgun.

GIL 2. I'm sorry.

PERRY. I sell insurance now. To farmers, mostly. Don't help much. *(Another pause.)*

GIL 2. Thanks, in any case, um … for your tolerance.

PERRY. Don't have to like what you tolerate. That's what toleration's for. Just so long as it don't touch me. *(As Perry speaks, Ray 2 appears. Gil sees him, but Perry doesn't at first.)*

RAY 2. Why's your friend out in the field?

GIL 2. He's cooling off.

RAY 2. Gonna take a lot of cooling. *(An awkward beat. Both men look at Perry expectantly.)*

PERRY. Oh! I'll, um … I'll just go keep an eye on him. You be all right, Ray?

RAY 2. I'll be fine. *(Reluctantly, Perry leaves. Ray 2 stares at Gil 2.)*

RAY 2. What's his name again? Out there?

GIL 2. Kit.

RAY 2. "Kit"? That what you made him out of?

GIL 2. He's sharing my life right now. I'm not surprised you forgot his name.

RAY 2. It was sort of hard to hear while we were dragging him from under the pews.

GIL 2. I'm so sorry for that. I never meant to —

RAY 2. Jesus Christ, Gil. What in hell are you doing? What are you doing? *(After a beat.)* How can you be with that?

GIL 2. You don't even know him.

RAY 2. I know he's half your age.

GIL 2. You think I should be with someone appropriate?

RAY 2. Yes!

GIL 2. Like Molly? *(As Ray 2 gives him a hard stare.)* We're really kind of an adorable couple. You should come visit us sometime.

RAY 2. I don't think so.

GIL 2. We're very quiet at home. He wants to move, and I don't — that's about the biggest issue. See, we live in Brooklyn Center, but he wants to live in the real Brooklyn. That's what he calls it, the "real" Brooklyn. I tell him, "You want the West Village, not Brooklyn. They're out in the Village — fighting for their rights, walking hand in hand." Anyway, he weeps and moans, but I won't move. His one dream, New York — and I won't go. *(With a smile.)* Other than that, we're perfect. *(After a beat.)* When we're done fighting we usually distract ourselves by making this beautiful imitation of love. It's really impressive. Convincing, I mean. There are times I almost believe it myself. There are times … *(Shrugging.)* Who knows what'll happen? Someday he'll probably go to New York without me. He's not a Midwesterner at heart. Not like us.

RAY 2. You'd be lucky to be rid of him.

GIL 2. You think so? Once he said — I didn't even prompt him — he said, "Everyone settles. Everyone." You think that's true? I don't. I think even in Kit's brain, somewhere deep in back — and believe me, there is somewhere deep in back — he's got a vision: glowing faces, couples walking up and down Sixth Avenue in the Village on a Sunday morning, carrying the newspaper, a book for later. The sun slanting down, turning it all into a river of bright dreams.

RAY 2. I thought he wanted to go to Brooklyn.

GIL 2. He'll figure it out. Of course, I suppose there are a lot of men who'd be delighted to have someone to settle for at all. Not Kit, though. He's too beautiful. So am I. So are you. We shouldn't have to settle.

RAY 2. I'm a married man.

GIL 2. Does your son know about me?

RAY 2. No.

GIL 2 He really wanted to kill me today.

RAY 2. I wanted to kill you myself. I haven't seen you in twenty-five years, and this is how you — ?

GIL 2. I said I'm sorry —

RAY 2.  Sorry? For Christ's sake, what were you thinking?! Why on earth did you come up here?

GIL 2.  Twenty-five years. It has been that, hasn't it? And every week, for twenty-five years, you wrote me a letter. What were you thinking?

RAY 2.  Those letters were about how I could *not* be with you.

GIL 2.  "I cannot be with you." Once a week, every week, twenty-five years. They came no matter what. Even after you got married and asked me to stop writing back. Made no difference. The letters kept coming. Monday morning: "How about that? A letter from Ray."

RAY 2.  They were a kind of meditation. Like writing in a journal.

GIL 2.  Oh, I was supposed to meditate? Didn't realize. "I love you, Gil" — that was in every letter. Was I supposed to meditate on that? Or how about, "Gil, you should see the hillside behind Logan's Drug. It's covered in wild roses."

RAY 2.  Why are you here?

GIL 2.  First, I apologize for what happened at the wedding rehearsal. I had no idea that was today, and I had *no* idea that Kit would —

RAY 2.  *Why are you here?!*

GIL 2.  Isn't it obvious? You stopped writing. *(They freeze. Lights shift. Ray 3 enters. His left arm and leg are slightly stiff — as though from a stroke. His speech is not affected. He stares at Gil 2.)*

RAY 3.  *(To audience.)* I still love him — the memory of him. His hands — smooth, the opposite of mine. He never belonged to this place the way I did. He wasn't raised on a farm; he lived in town, as much as he lived anywhere. In his head — that's where Gil lived: outside town, a thousand miles past all the farms. Nowhere else would've been safe. *(As he continues, they exit slowly.)* It was different for me. I got along. To me, everyone looked good. Everyone looked ... fascinating. I had a natural instinct for asking people about themselves — the secret of being popular. I had girlfriends in high school, a few. By the time I was a senior, I was going with Molly Stensrud. *(After a beat.)* Me and Molly were the all-star couple in high-school. When my folks died, she was with me all the time. Only person I could talk to. She felt comfortable, she felt ... right. And the way people looked at us on the street. The smiles that came ... I felt like a hero. We had the whole town rooting for us. I knew who I was going to marry. I was already working the farm I'd inherit when Anson died. Then — right about then — I asked the wrong person about himself. *(Ray 3 exits the way he came. Ray enters in spotlight.)*

RAY. *(To audience.)* The first time, I wasn't drunk. It wasn't way late at night. I wasn't scared. It was my idea. Gil would never have suggested it. He probably thought he was lucky out of his mind just to have somebody to confide in. Confess to, more like it. I had to lie and tell him I had a cousin who was queer, so he'd trust me enough. Not that he'd ever done anything with anybody. But you know, he had all these fantasies about everyone and stuff. I was the first he ever told. We spent a whole afternoon on a rock by the river, him telling me all this dirty stuff. Only it wasn't dirty. It was just like how gorgeous he thought these stupid football players were. I just kept listening to him. That afternoon, and the next and the next ... *(A beat.)* That's how you fall in love. One confession at a time. *(Ray exits. Action continues as lights crossfade to:)*

## Scene 3

*2001. Late afternoon. There's still sunlight, some coming through large holes in the roof. Ray 3, wearing a sportscoat over his overalls, walks cautiously into the house, as though worried about rotting boards. Indeed, on one step the floor creaks dangerously. He steps to the left — even worse. To the right — still bad. He circles closer to the wall where the floor is stronger. That's okay. Ray 3 makes his way to the middle of the room where he stands silently, taking in the continuing slow ruin of the place.*

RAY 3. *(Calling.)* Jody. *Jo-dy!!* *(After a moment, his grandson Jody enters, carrying three nylon fold-out camp stools.)* Where in hell were you? Can't even keep up with an old man.

JODY.  I was getting these. Where do you want 'em? *(Jody moves toward Ray 3, automatically taking the route by the wall.)*

RAY 3.  How come you knew where to walk?

JODY.  I come here all the time.

RAY 3.  What for?

JODY.  Hey — I'm seventeen.

RAY 3.  *(As Jody sets up the stools.)* What's that supposed to mean?

JODY.  What you don't know won't hurt you.

RAY 3.  Does Ray Junior know you come here?

JODY.  Dad and I are on a need-to-know basis. Is this how you want 'em?

RAY 3.  Not so close together.

JODY.  Don't know why I have to be here.

RAY 3.  I want you here.

JODY.  Don't see why.

RAY 3.  'Cause I do! Stop being a smart-ass.

JODY.  Why don't I get a stool?

RAY 3.  'Cause you're not an adult. Kids should hover. Just hover around, so they can beat it at a moment's notice. Did you guys do all this damage?

JODY.  What guys?

RAY 3.  You and your buddies. Whoever in hell you bring out here. You completely wrecked the roof.

JODY.  Try nature? It's called maintenance, Old One. When's the last time you were here?

RAY 3.  Before you were born. Don't know why your father hasn't torn it down by now.

JODY.  You shouldn't have given it to him.

RAY 3.  It was time. Farm was too much for me.

JODY.  You shouldn't have given him everything. He makes you live like shit.

RAY 3.  Watch your mouth. Help me sit down. *(Jody helps Ray 3 sit in a stool. Ray 3 could have managed, but this is easier.)* Where is it?

JODY.  Where's what? *(As Ray 3 gives him a don't-be-an-idiot look.)* It's in the truck.

RAY 3.  What'd you leave it there for? You don't leave something like that alone. Go get it!

JODY.  *(Circling out of the room, toward the front door.)* It's not the end of life —

RAY 3. That's exactly what it is! Be careful with it, you irreverent little —

JODY. *(Exiting.)* But then he was gone! *(The front door slams — not angrily. Ray 3 stares at the room. Unconsciously, he rubs his left arm. He notices what he's doing, stares at the arm, then slaps it hard.)*

RAY 3. Shit!

JODY. *(Off. From the porch outside.)* Watch your mouth!

RAY 3. *Get the damn thing!*

JODY. *(Off.)* He's here! *(Sound of Jody running off the porch as Ray 3 struggles to rise. Before he does, Reese appears in the archway. In his forties, Reese is dressed casually. He looks every bit the grade-school teacher he is. Ray 3 sits back down when he sees who it is.)*

REESE. Hello, Ray. Sorry I'm late.

RAY 3. That's okay, Reese. Glad you found it.

REESE. Should've been easy, I suppose. Not that many abandoned farmhouses left out here. Guess they need the acreage, eh?

RAY 3. Guess someone does.

REESE. The fields go on forever and ever. *(Reese takes a step toward Ray 3. The floor creaks. Ray 3 gestures him to go around. Reese does so, moving to the area with the three stools.)* You ever gonna tear this place down?

RAY 3. I won't. My son will. This fall.

REESE. How long did you live in it?

RAY 3. I didn't.

REESE. Oh? Who did?

RAY 3. Nobody.

REESE. Nobody ever? Why was it built?

RAY 3. Gil should be here soon. Sorry he's late. *(Reese decides not to pursue it. He sits. A moment passes. Reese sighs deeply.)* Glad it's almost through?

REESE. *(Nodding.)* It's been an odyssey, I'll tell you that. My wife has no idea why I'm doing this. Chasing all over the country. He wasn't even my relative, by blood. He was her uncle. Nobody on her side wants to know anything about the past. Can you believe that? Perfectly willing to let a relative just flake off, forget him … I've become the family historian by default. Don't know why I like doing it. Putting the pieces together, like a jigsaw puzzle. Harlow

I never would've found if you hadn't answered my ad. You made a real sacrifice, I'll give you that.

RAY 3. He wasn't much of a man.

REESE. Hm?

RAY 3. Harlow.

REESE. *(With a soft laugh.)* I know that. But he was my uncle, by marriage. He went missing, and he deserved to be counted. *(A beat.)* Alcoholism is a disease, you know. In a way he couldn't help himself.

RAY 3. How do you know? He died ten years before you were born.

REESE. I just have a feeling about it.

RAY 3. He tried to kill me. He could've helped that. *(Jody reenters. He carries a funeral urn. Without a word, he circles the room with it, then places it on the floor.)*

JODY. That okay?

RAY 3. Fine. *(Jody, not quite sure what to do, finally sits on the remaining stool. Reese speaks to him.)*

REESE. I'm a teacher. Sixth grade. It's a great age. Kids just starting to glimpse a world that's wider than their neighborhood. Have you ever been to Denver? It's a beautiful town. My wife and I take the kids backpacking all the time. They love it. We have three kids. Huey, Dewey and Louie. No, I'm kidding. Jenny, Julian and Max. Max is from Korea. He's adopted. I don't know, somehow we felt we just wanted to share how happy we were with somebody who wouldn't have had a life, you know? We've always been glad we did it. *(A beat.)* 'Course he's hitting puberty now and ... But he's gonna be fine. They all go through that cultural anxiety thing, you know? That, that, um ... terror sort of thing. They look in the mirror, they're not — But he is. Max really is. He fits in perfectly. Just doesn't know it yet. *(A longer beat. They stare at the urn.)* 'Course, Harlow never had any children. That we know of. *(They freeze. Lights shift. Ray 3, Jody and Reese rise, fold their stools and exit directly across the room — no creaking floor. Jody also takes the urn. At the same time, Ray enters and speaks to the audience.)*

RAY. Anson finally told me what happened to Gil. I was glad Gil only got a year. Everybody said the workhouse was better than St. Cloud prison. Gil should've got a medal for shooting Lewis. For years

Lewis walked up and down Main with that hand with two missing fingers, claiming girls "like it better." *(A beat.)* I wrote Gil that I thought it was better if he didn't come back. Anson told me I shouldn't write Gil anymore after that. I tried to stop. I really did. I couldn't, though. So in every letter I always made sure to say, "Don't come back. It's bad for you. Being special's bad for you. It'll be bad for you your whole life." *(Ray exits the way he came. As he does so, Ray 2 enters a spot to begin another "letter.")*

RAY 2. Dear Gil. I was elected mayor today. Can you believe it? Everybody here thinks I have the perfect life. But I think the only perfect life is yours. You're the only one who knows what both our lives are like. I wonder why you always send me your new address whenever you move. You could disappear — sometimes I wish you would. I could walk back into my house, full of my perfect life, stare at my perfect family. *(A beat.)* Ever been in a city where you don't speak the language? Everybody looks normal enough, but when they start talking ... That's what it's like in my house. Emotional sign language. I think you have the perfect life. *(Ray 2 exits. Action continues as lights go very briefly to black.)*

## Scene 4

*1948. Lights bump up to reveal Harlow and Gil as they were at the end of Scene 1. Harlow holds the straight razor to Gil's throat. Ray is nowhere to be seen.*

HARLOW. He better find that gun.

GIL. Get off me!

HARLOW. You don't want me to get off you. You like it. Isn't that right, you fucking little fairy — you *like* it!

GIL. *(Struggling.)* Please — !! *(Harlow suddenly grabs Gil by the hair and makes a quick, shallow cut on Gil's neck with the razor. Gil screams.)*

HARLOW. *(Shouting over the screaming.)* How do you like that!?

Huh?! You like that, you little cocksucking piece of shit!!? I ought to drain you like a pig! *(Harlow's stopped cutting him, but Gil, terrified, keeps screaming.)* You thought you were gonna be the one hurtin' people tonight? That what you thought?

GIL. Please don't kill me.

HARLOW. Why not? What you got to live for? *(A beat.) What!!?* I got nothing to live for, ain't got a penny in my pocket, but at least I'm a human being. You'll never know what that feels like. *(Lifting the razor to show Gil his blood.)* See that? That's your fag's blood. Know how many faggots I've killed? Go on, guess. *Guess!!*

GIL. One?

HARLOW. Hell, more'n that!

GIL. I don't know.

HARLOW. *(Razor to Gil's throat again.)* If you ain't gonna play the game —

GIL. No — ! I am! I am! Five?

HARLOW. *(Going through Gil's pockets.)* That's right! See? You got it right away! People pretend there ain't any fags at all, but I know better. I see 'em all the time. I ride the boxcars with 'em. I camp with 'em. I even let 'em come on to me. Then, when no one's looking —

GIL. *Why?!*

HARLOW. 'Cause you're a mistake, that's why! Think I wanna live in a universe where God makes mistakes!? *Why ain't you got any money?!*

GIL. These aren't my clothes! My stuff's over there. *(Gil points at the pile of his wet clothes. Harlow leans over, trying to reach it. As he does so, Gil suddenly kicks him off, grabbing for the razor at the same time. The two of them struggle on the floor for the razor. Ray appears in the archway. He carries the gun, a revolver, at his side. At just that moment, Harlow slugs Gil hard, stunning him.)*

HARLOW. *(To Gil.)* Don't you *ever* touch me!! *(Noticing Ray for the first time, with complete calm.)* Good, you found the gun. 'Bout time. Give it here. *(Ray slowly raises the gun and points it at Harlow.)*

RAY. Why's he bleeding?

HARLOW. 'Cause I cut him, why do you think? Gonna cut him a lot more, too. Gonna cut you.

RAY. *(As Harlow, still holding the razor, starts toward him.)* Stop. Stop! I'll kill you!

25

GIL. Ray — !

HARLOW. *(Stopping.)* One time I killed a man, took me three hours. Hit him over the head with a brick. He kept waking up — I'd hit him again. I'd think he was dead, he'd wake up, I just kept hitting him. Finally you couldn't recognize his face — *(Harlow suddenly lunges for the gun. He and the surprised Ray struggle over it as Gil tries to grab the razor again. Harlow, who seems to relish these fights, smacks Gil hard with a wide backhand, sending Gil to the floor. Then he trips Ray, wrestling the gun away as Ray falls. Harlow stands over them with a weapon in either hand.)*

HARLOW. You two keep it secret, don't you?

GIL. What do you think?

HARLOW. Don't talk like that to me! I may be down on my luck, but I ain't so low as you. *(Harlow kicks Gil.)*

RAY. *Hey — !!*

HARLOW. Gimme the keys for that truck!

RAY. *(Tossing him the keys.)* Take 'em! Take 'em and go.

HARLOW. Gimme your belt. *Give* it! *(Ray takes off his belt. Harlow grabs it, forces Ray facedown on the floor and ties Ray's hands behind his back. He also takes Ray's wallet.)* I want you to know if you weren't fairies, I wouldn't kill you. I'm not a homicidal maniac or nothing. But see, fags are different. Nobody minds when you die. They're relieved. They feel better when you're gone. *(Gil tries to make a break, but Harlow trains the gun on him.)* You can have it fast or slow, kid! *(Gil lies back down. Harlow quickly rifles the pile of Gil's clothes, looking for valuables. All the pockets are empty.)* You know, I got secrets too. Told your little friend here while you were out.

GIL. He's killed people. Five —

RAY. Oh, God. Oh, help us, God —

HARLOW. Don't you dare pray to God! Pray to me! Pray to *me!* *(With a chuckle.)* Want to know the first one I killed? My cousin. Couldn't believe he was in my family. Made him disappear. They still don't know what happened to the little queer. And you know what? They don't care. *(To Gil, pointing at the pile of clothes.)* Grab that. *(To Ray.)* You got a shovel in that truck? *(No answer. Harlow puts the gun to Ray's temple.)* You got a shovel!!?

RAY. *Yes!*

26

HARLOW. *(Pulling them up.)* Good. 'Cause you got some digging to do. *(Harlow shoves the two boys ahead of him toward the front of the house. As they disappear through the archway there's a sudden sickening, dull thud. Harlow, bleeding from his forehead, staggers back into the room and falls unconscious on the floor. After a beat, Ray and Gil creep back into the living room. Behind them comes Anson, an Old Testament–looking man with a fierce look on his face — and a shovel in his hand.)*

ANSON. What'd he say his name was? *(They freeze. Lights go to black very briefly, and they exit. A spot suddenly discovers Ray 2 standing in the now-empty room. He begins a "letter.")*

RAY 2. Dear Gil, I stopped writing you for a reason. I resent having to write one more letter. I always thought I loved you — that I'd be able to forgive whatever you said or did. But I can't. I never want to hear from you. I certainly never want to hear Kit's name again. I'm going to try to make the second half of my life better — more honest. I advise you to do the same. I'm sorry I even have memories of you. Ray. *(Action continues as lights crossfade to:)*

## Scene 5

*1973. Ray 2 looks out the window. Gil 2 kneels on all fours, examining the floor.*

RAY 2. Look at Perry with that horrible little kid of yours. What on earth you think they're talking about?

GIL 2. Kit's very well-read in certain areas. What's Perry know about lingerie?

RAY 2. If they're talking flannel, everything. Perry can sit and listen to anybody about anything. Listens to all sides, too. That's pretty rare up here — well, you know. Doesn't always tip his hand, either. It was three years before I knew what he thought of me and Molly getting married.

GIL 2. Maybe we should've died here. Like a pair of great lovers.

I can still see my blood. I think.

RAY 2. *(Still looking out the window.)* Most patient man I know.

GIL 2. Who?

RAY 2. Perry. Haven't you been listening?

GIL 2. Haven't you?

RAY 2. I can see why you want to be with me. It's like we're married already.

GIL 2. Like we always have been. *(As Ray 2 turns away.)* We'd be such a great couple. We wouldn't have to live in Brooklyn Center. I wouldn't make you do that.

RAY 2. We sure couldn't live here.

GIL 2. We'd go to New York; we'd both be lost. We'd be this aging gay couple, holding hands on the sidewalk, no matter how corny it looked — except at night, when the kids from Jersey with the baseball bats show up.

RAY 2. Where do you get all this?

GIL 2. I read.

RAY 2. Believe me, you're making New York sound *real* attractive.

GIL 2. It is! You can say, "I'm gay," and — in general — they won't kill you. They really won't. *(Ray gives him a rueful smile.)*

RAY 2. Not many farms in Manhattan.

GIL 2. There are one or two fine parcels of land left in the Village. They're perhaps a bit smaller than what you have here —

RAY 2. It'd be tough to get by on anything smaller.

GIL 2. We'll supplement. I'll take in laundry.

RAY 2. How'm I going to get the heavy equipment there?

GIL 2. Drive?

RAY 2. Down the freeway?

GIL 2. On the shoulder. No problem's too big.

RAY 2. Guess not. Where'll I put all my personal things?

GIL 2. Personal things?

RAY 2. You know — wife, son ... *(Gil goes silent. If he's on the floor he rises.)*

GIL 2. Trunk. Open it up once a year on Christmas.

RAY 2. Doesn't sound too fair —

GIL 2. *I was there first.*

RAY 2. No, you weren't. I was going with Molly —

GIL 2. *(Poking Ray 2 gently in the chest.)* I was there. First. *(A beat.)* Why'd you stop writing to me?

RAY 2.  My son's getting married.

GIL 2.  So?

RAY 2.  Twenty-five years. What was I doing? Who I was doing it for? I didn't know anymore. I couldn't ... Nobody can live on that, Gil. It's a ghost. *(After a beat.)* Besides, I have to be a family man. I have to be for them, or I'm not ... for them.

GIL 2.  Hard to be articulate when you don't believe what you're saying.

RAY 2.  I don't expect you to understand —

GIL 2.  Why? 'Cause I didn't make a fake family?

RAY 2.  *It's not fake!*

GIL 2.  You are. Every week, when you write that letter, you are fake. No, I take it back. That's the one time you're genuine.

RAY 2.  What we had was over a long time ago —

GIL 2.  It's not over. You know, maybe I wish it was over too, but it isn't.

RAY 2.  Gil —

GIL 2.  If it was over, you'd have shoved Kit and me back in our car and told us to get the hell out. But you didn't. Look where we are, Ray. Look where we're standing.

RAY 2.  *(Turning away from him.)* You know the kind of questions that are going through my family's minds right now?

GIL 2.  I'm sorry.

RAY 2.  You destroyed that rehearsal. I suppose I'm lucky you didn't stumble in here tomorrow and ruin the real thing.

GIL 2.  I don't pretend I know what I'm doing here. Any more than you know — really — why you stopped writing. All I know is that I have questions. About us. I need the answers. You know, it's totally different out there. The way we grew up ... here ... you're right, we probably couldn't have done it, but now ... I can be a person out there. So can you. And it's only going to get better —

RAY 2.  You're with Kit.

GIL 2.  And you're with Molly, but I don't see them here.

RAY 2.  I can't rip up everyone's life around me.

GIL 2.  You're better off lying to them?

RAY 2.  *Why not?* It was better to lie. She earned that lie. All she's ever done is love me. *(A beat.)* I won't leave them. I won't leave my son.

GIL 2. He's a grown man. He's getting married. Besides, he hates people like us.

RAY 2. Ray Junior's his own person — all right? I mean, you walk in unannounced with that … that creature —

GIL 2. He's not a "creature" —

RAY 2. My son's never seen anybody like that, he's never been around —

GIL 2. And that gives him the right to throw Kit over a pew? What the hell kind of values did he grow up with, Ray?

RAY 2. *Our* values! This town's values! I did what I could, I told him everyone's a human being; that doesn't mean he has to listen to me. He's got his own mind. I can't change that — I *wouldn't* change it. Why in hell did you bring Kit in the first place!?

GIL 2. I didn't want to. He insisted. He lives with me, Ray. You think I can hide how I feel? He's jealous, and he's just trying to fuck everything up in his own, adorable little way.

RAY 2. And he doesn't matter to you?

GIL 2. I don't know. That's what I'm saying. That's why I'm here. I want to find out, I want to *know*, if you and I can —

RAY 2. We can't. *(After a beat.)* We won't. You and Kit get in your car. Get out of here. *(As Ray 2 starts for the front door, Gil 2 sits down on the floor. Ray 2 looks back.)* Gil —

GIL 2. God sees us, Ray.

RAY 2. Will you get up? *(Instead, Gil 2 lies on his back, staring up.)*

GIL 2. God sees us.

RAY 2. When did you get religion?

GIL 2. I didn't. But God sees what He made. I don't need religion to know that. *(Holding his hand above him, studying it.)* My body is religion. Each cell. What I know in each cell. It's all we are: billions — trillions? — of cells. Each one with a wall. Each and every one. Trillions of walls. That's what we're mostly made up of: walls.

RAY 2. Some of us are mostly made up of horseshit.

GIL 2. But which ones? *(After a beat.)* Say you don't love me. Say it. I'll go. *(A silence.)*

RAY 2. Some nights, when Molly's asleep — in the same room, in the same bed where you and I first … I'll get up, and … I'll go downstairs. I have to walk way on the far edges of the steps so they don't creak, and … eventually I'll get downstairs. And I'll see the living room. You remember that day in the living room.

GIL 2. Yes.

RAY 2. And if it's summer I'll go out on the porch. And I'll just sit there on the rail, where we sat. That night you first held my hand. In the dark. For an hour. *(A beat.)* And then I'll go back upstairs to bed. Some nights, I can even fall asleep again.*(A beat.)* In the morning Molly's always so pretty. Always so rested. She has so much energy.

GIL 2. Molly's a strong woman.

RAY 2. She is.

GIL 2. She'd survive losing you.

RAY 2. *(Turning away from him.)* You don't know a thing about it. I married her. We had a son. That's it — that's my life. I take care of them.

GIL 2. You also take care of an abandoned house. *(After a beat.)* What if it comes out?

RAY 2. What?

GIL 2. You and me.

RAY 2. It's not going to come out —

GIL 2. I could make it come out.

RAY 2. If you did that, you'd never hear from me again.

GIL 2. What have I got to lose?

RAY 2. She'd never believe you.

GIL 2. I have your letters, Ray. I brought them with me. Boxes and boxes.

RAY 2. You didn't. *(They freeze. Lights shift. Ray enters and begins a "letter.")*

RAY. Nothing to do around here.

GIL 2. Every week …

RAY. Wind chill's about thirty-five below, which isn't that bad.

GIL 2. Twenty-five years …

RAY. But it's snowing again.

GIL 2. "It's Monday … "

RAY. I'm waiting to plow the driveway down to the mailbox so I can send this.

GIL 2. "Look — a letter from Ray." *(Gil 2 and Ray 2 slowly exit.)*

RAY. Family's been in all day. Molly's writing more childrens' stories. She's getting published, so she must be good. Ray Junior's

31

really active. Once he learns to walk, he's gonna be all over. *(A beat.)* Remember the day we stared at the snow out my bedroom window? And no matter how hard we looked, we couldn't tell where the sky ended and the field began? *(Lights crossfade as Ray exits. In transition light Ray 3, Jody and Reese return to their Scene Three positions with their stools and the urn.)*

## Scene 6

*2001. Lights up on Ray 3, Jody and Reese staring at the urn as before. A silence, then sound of Gil 3 singing in the yard. He's singing in a foreign language, but it's clear he's a little drunk, slurring his words. The tune is stately, muted by the distance. No one in the room rises, though Reese and Jody seem surprised. Ray 3, on the other hand, doesn't.*

GIL 3. *(Off.)* "Du gamla, Du fria, Du fjallhoga Nord, du tysta, du gladjerika skona! Jag halsar dig vanaste land uppa jord din sol, din himmel, dina angder grona! Din sol, din himmel, dina angder grona!
REESE. Is that him?
RAY 3. Yeah.
JODY. What's he singing?
RAY 3. The Swedish national anthem. *(As Gil 3 draws closer to the house, the Scandanavian origin of the song becomes more apparent. As he enters the front door he continues the song, but in English.)*
GIL 3. *(Singing.)* "Thy throne is the mem'ry of great days of yore, when all through the world thy name was carried, thou art this, I know, the same as of old. In thee I'll live, in thee I'll die, O North Land, In thee I'll live, in thee I'll die, O North Land." *(As Gil 3 sings he appears in the archway. He moves toward them. The floor is weak beneath him. Still singing, he arcs around to the stool Jody's using. Jody gets up, surrendering his seat to Gil 3. As Gil 3 sits he finishes his stately, soulful rendition of the song. As they stare at him, Gil 3 fixes on the urn at his feet. He kicks it over, spilling the ashes.)*

32

RAY 3.  Gil — !

REESE.  What in the — ?! *(Reese is instantly down on his knees, scooping ashes back into the urn as the others look on.)*

JODY.  Should I help?

GIL 3.  *No!*

REESE.  No thanks, that's all right. I'll … I've got it.

GIL 3.  Got *him,* you mean.

RAY 3.  Gil.

GIL 3.  Don't "Gil" me! You know how many ashes I've scattered? You have no idea how many … *Good* people!

RAY 3.  That's not the point. This is our responsibility —

GIL 3.  Responsibility?! To that?! To Harlow? *(With a disgusted snort.)* You know he looks better this way.

RAY 3.  *Gil — !*

REESE.  It's all right.

GIL 3.  I can't believe you answered his ad.

RAY 3.  I did. I did answer his ad, and I answered all his questions, and the coroner's questions and the judge's questions — and I finally found you again, and got you to come here so you could answer all the damn questions too. And I'm not apologizing for that, Gil. You know I did the right thing. *(As Gil 3 gives him a hard look.)* Anyway, it's over now, and it's time to scatter Harlow. Let's just get it done, and you can get in your damn car and get the hell out of here.

GIL 3.  It's a crappy urn.

RAY 3.  Shut up! *(Reese finishes his task, replaces the urn where it was and sits facing it. With Jody standing behind them, they all stare at the urn.)*

REESE.  *(Beginning a prayer.)* Lord —

GIL 3.  Oh, *God* — !! I can't do this!

REESE.  *(Reaching for his coat pocket.)* Do you need to see the court order? *(Gil groans.)*

RAY 3.  We have to do this ceremony. It's part of the agreement.

GIL 3.  *(To Jody.)* Thanks to your grandfather, we're now on probation.

REESE.  Lord, a terrible crime occurred many years ago on this spot — on this farm. You saw fit to take my Uncle Harlow before I could ever know him —

GIL 3.  You were lucky.

REESE.  *(Hand going for the pocket again.)* Respectful. The order said respectful.

GIL 3.  All right, all right ...

REESE.  You saw fit to let the crime and the criminals who perpetrated it lie hidden for all these years in their sin —

GIL 3.  I'm *not* going to be called a sinner — !

RAY 3.  Gil! Just let it be! We killed his uncle!

GIL 3.  *Anson* killed him.

RAY 3.  You knew about it. So did I.

GIL 3.  Yeah, and the difference is, I didn't open my big mouth!

RAY 3.  I want to be free of this. You have to help me be free of this.

GIL 3.  Why?! Why should I help you be forgiven? Twenty years I tried to get you to forgive me. I don't recall that working.

RAY 3.  I'm sorry.

GIL 3.  Oh — now you're sorry. Thanks, that's a tremendous comfort.

REESE.  *(Beginning the prayer again.)* Lord —

GIL 3.  Worst years of my life, I wrote you every week — twice a week sometimes. I buried a generation of friends and lovers, and what did you care? You're up here on your farm, safe — same as always.

RAY 3.  Not like always.

REESE.  *Can we please get on with it?*

GIL 3.  Yeah, yeah — go ahead.

RAY 3.  *(Simultaneously.)* Sure, fine.

REESE.  Lord —

GIL 3.  *(To Ray 3)* Whole town knows about you now anyway. Hell, your own grandkid knows. Jody, you know your Grandpa's a queer?

JODY.  Yeah. So?

GIL 3.  Do you care?

JODY.  Not really.

GIL 3.  Think your Grandma would've cared?

JODY.  I don't know. She's been dead for —

GIL 3.  Exactly. Nobody cares, Ray. You're out, and nobody cares. You should've forgiven me.

RAY 3.  *(After a silence.)* Can we please — ?

34

GIL 3. Yeah, sure. Why not?

REESE. Lord. The ways of salvation in men's hearts are often long and winding. Harlow I believe was seeking your love in the only way he could.

GIL 3. Oh, for ...

REESE. I know You don't condemn Harlow for having fallen to a low condition. I know You would not keep so unfortunate a man from You for all eternity. Harlow sinned, perhaps very greatly. But he sought an answer, and love in a world that didn't really know how to love him. *(Gil 3 rolls his eyes — and maybe his whole head — at this one. But he holds his tongue.)* Thank You, Lord, for the gift of Harlow. Thank you for the miracle of his discovery, and an end to the mystery that has plagued his family for so long. Each man deserves to be counted, and today we count Harlow.

GIL 3. Today we *spread* Harlow.

REESE. That does it! I'm going back to the judge!

RAY 3. Reese, you don't have to —

REESE. I mean it! You can sit in jail! Both of you! *(Reese picks up the urn.)*

RAY 3. Please, please, please — Jody, help me up. *(As Jody does so.)* Gil feels a little victimized here. By me, I mean. You can understand that. Why don't you and Jody take the urn out in the field and start scattering? Let me talk some sense into him. It should be a solemn thing out there. Jody can help you.

REESE. It's not what the order says.

RAY 3. Help us out. We've gone through quite a bit. We just need a little forgiveness here, that's all.

REESE. *(With a sigh.)* All right. I'll forgive you this much, even if God won't.

GIL 3. What's that mean?

RAY 3. Leave it alone!

GIL 3. No, what do you mean by that? "God won't"?

REESE. Simply that He won't, that's all. He won't. You're homosexuals.

GIL 3. What?

RAY 3. *(Trying to move Reese and Jody out.)* None of it matters —

REESE. Of course it does. It gives me no comfort to point it out, but you're both homosexuals. God won't forgive that. Not unless

35

you renounce it for the unspeakable sin it is. Are you ready to do that? *(After a silence.)* So you'll never see God. You'll be damned for eternity.

GIL 3. For eternity?

REESE. I'm sorry.

RAY 3. Okay. Out you two go, then —

GIL 3. Harlow will see God, but we won't?

REESE. Yes. It gives me no comfort to say it.

GIL 3. I don't believe it.

RAY 3. Gil, just let —

GIL 3. This *fucker* says I won't see God?!

REESE. It gives me no —

GIL 3. I *better* fucking see God! After what I've been through? I *better* see Him!

RAY 3. Stop it! *(To the others.)* Will you two just *go?!*

REESE. The judge'll get a full report of this. A full report!

GIL 3. Yeah, well tell St. Peter, too! And tell him I'm gonna *kick his ass!!* (Reese and Jody exit with the urn, circling carefully by the wall. Ray 3 shoves Gil 3 towards his stool.)

RAY 3. Sit down! *(Gil 3 does so, starts to sing softly — the same song as before.)*

GIL 3. "Du gamla, Du fria, Du fjällhoga Nord — "

RAY 3. And I do not need to hear the Swedish anthem again.

GIL 3. Why not? My parents sang it. It gave them strength.

RAY 3. Not forever; they're dead. Knock it off.

GIL 3. I *will* see God. So will you. *He* won't, but we will. *(A silence. Gil 3 can't meet his disapproving gaze. Ray 3 breaks off and looks out the window.)*

RAY 3. Look at that: they're headed right to where we buried him. Same part of the field. There's something vindictive in that guy, definitely.

GIL 3. I can't believe you helped him.

RAY 3. Neither can I. *(Sighing.)* Just as well, though. There comes a time when you have to tell the truth.

GIL 3. Like you told the truth to Molly?

RAY 3. *(Unable to meet his gaze.)* Had to wait for Molly to … you know.

GIL 3. The final fig leaf. *(Ray 3 looks out the window.)*

RAY 3. I had to wait for Molly. *(They freeze. Lights shift. Gil enters and begins a "letter." As he does, Gil 3 and Ray 3 slowly exit straight out.)*

GIL. Dear Ray. Thanks for writing. No one else does, not even my family. 'Course, who expected them to, right? I was scared when I first got here. The "workhouse." Bad stuff does happen here, I won't lie to you. Nothing I can't survive, I guess. *(After a beat.)* Ray? I was thinking: when Anson dies, maybe I could move back? Just a thought. I don't mean to pressure you. *(After a beat.)* I know you don't want to move, but really, if we both went down to the Cities or wherever, we could do anything we want. We could get rooms in the same building. No one would have to know. No one would have to know anything. We'd just be gone, you know? And together, and … alive. *(Gil exits. Action continues as lights crossfade to:)*

## Scene 7

*1948. Only moments have elapsed since Anson struck Harlow. Anson hunkers over Harlow, who's still unconscious. The shovel's on the floor at Anson's side. Gil frees Ray's hands from the belt.*

ANSON. Tie him up. *(Gil quickly moves to Harlow and ties his hands behind his back.)* His name is Harlow?

RAY. That's what he said.

ANSON. You ever seen him around here before? Know anybody who has?

RAY. No, sir.

ANSON. Check his pockets. *(As Gil does so.)* He say anything else?

GIL. That he'd murdered people.

ANSON. He was gonna murder you?

RAY. Yes, sir. I believe he was. *(Gil pulls Ray's wallet and keys from Harlow's pocket. Grabbing them.)* Those are mine — he took 'em.

37

*(Gil pulls out the razor, searches further. He can't find anything else.)*
GIL. That's all there is.
ANSON. Not much to this man.
RAY. You going to take him in?
ANSON. In?
RAY. To the sheriff?
ANSON. Let's just think about that. What'll happen if I take him in?
GIL. He'll go to jail?
ANSON. What for?
GIL. Threatening us. And, and … robbing and hitting us and tying up Ray and he cut my neck —
ANSON. Let me see. *(Examining it.)* That's not dangerous.
GIL. It *felt* dangerous!
ANSON. So far, along with vagrancy, he's got maybe six months. What else? *(Forcefully.)* What else?! You can't say a man just wanted to kill you. Got to give a reason. Why'd he want to kill you? *(A nervous silence.)* Why was he calling you fairies? *(Ray and Gil look at each other, terrified at what Anson may have heard.)*
RAY. He wasn't.
GIL. No, he was saying some of the people he killed —
ANSON. *He was going to kill you 'cause he thought you were fairies. Why'd he think you were fairies?! (A beat.)* When he wakes up I can just ask him. *(A beat. Ray opens his mouth to speak.)*
GIL. I am.
RAY. Gil —
ANSON. You are what?
GIL. I am … one. A … fairy — not Ray, though. Just me. Honest.
ANSON. *(Moving to Gil, staring closely at him.)* You ever touch my grandson?
GIL. No, sir.
RAY. Grandpa, I —
ANSON. Quiet! *(To Gil.)* So he was gonna kill you 'cause he hates … people like you?
GIL. Yes.
ANSON. And he was gonna kill Ray 'cause he was here? 'Cause he was a witness?
GIL. I guess. *(Anson ponders this a moment. He half turns away*

*from Gil, then swings back with the razor open. He holds it against Gil's throat.)*

ANSON. Don't you *ever* lie to me!!

RAY. What are you *doing* — ?!

ANSON. *(To Ray.)* Did he ever touch you? *Did he ever touch you!?* Did you ever touch him!?

RAY. Grandpa — !

ANSON. Don't "Grandpa" me! You sneaked out! Middle of the night! Look where I find you! Look who I find you with! You don't respect this house!? You lie to me in this house? I know what I heard, boy! I know what I saw!

RAY. I only —

ANSON. *Did — you — ever — touch — him!?*

RAY. *Yes!*

ANSON. *(After a silence.)* More than once?

RAY. Last fall. All winter. *(Another silence.)*

ANSON. Is that what you are? Ray? Is that what you are?

RAY. I don't know. I don't think so —

ANSON. What do you think?!

RAY. *I don't know! (Harlow begins to stir. Anson moves to him, puts the gun to his ear.)*

ANSON. You gonna be any trouble?

HARLOW. No.

ANSON. You from around here?

HARLOW. No, sir. Passing through.

ANSON. Ever been this way before?

HARLOW. No, sir.

ANSON. Have any people up here?

HARLOW. My people are all out west. Do you have to point that at — ?

ANSON. Shut up! *(To Ray.)* Something's gonna be left, Ray. Your father took his own ... Took everything he could. But he didn't take you. I gotta believe there was a reason he didn't take you. Something's gonna be left when I die. Grab the shovel.

RAY. Grandpa —

ANSON. Grab it! *(As Ray reluctantly does so.)* You're gonna help me, understand? You're not gonna ask questions. I'll get you out of this mess, but you have to do what I say. You have to be strong.

You have to be a man. The memory of your mother and father is in your hands today. Your whole life is in your hands; you're not gonna throw it away on account of people like this. There's too much depending on you. Is that clear?

RAY. *(After a beat.)* Yes, sir.

ANSON. Follow us out, then. *(Kicking Harlow.)* Get up! *(With great difficulty, Harlow does so.)*

HARLOW. Listen, I was just trying to scare the boys —

ANSON. *(Pointing the gun directly at Harlow, cocking it.)* This can be your last moment on earth right now. *(Something in Harlow crumples. His eyes close and he slumps where he stands.)* Outside. *(Harlow heads out through the archway, with Anson following. As they disappear out the front door Ray hesitates.)*

RAY. Gil? Gil, are you — ?

ANSON. *(From outside.)* Come on!! *(Ray hurries outside with the shovel. For a long moment Gil is still. Then he moves to the window and freezes as lights shift and Gil 2 enters. Gil 2 addresses the audience.)*

GIL 2. Ray was already digging a hole. Anson had the gun. Harlow … *(Suddenly there's the sound of a shot outside.)* Only one bullet. One bullet, one hole, one hole in the ground and then — no holes at all. Nothing. The fields went on forever. No one in sight. And, for miles and miles, no one who'd ever heard of Harlow. *(Gil 2 exits the way he came. Lights shift again: Gil begins a "letter.")*

GIL. Ray? I was sorry to hear that Anson died. Honest. He was your Grandpa, despite whatever else he was. I know I said I'd stop writing, and I will if that's what you want. I understand. You're married now, kid on the way. So it's okay — I understand. Honest. Almost out of school now. Can't believe it. Time to work in the real world. Got to admit I sometimes wonder, though. Is there a real world? I love you. *(Gil exits. Action continues as lights crossfade to:)*

## Scene 8

*1973. Ray 2 and Gil 2 as they were at the end of Act One, Scene 5.*

RAY 2. You did not bring those letters.
GIL 2. Actually, I did. Glad I took the hatchback. They just fill it up. *(Ray 2 hesitates, then takes a step or two toward the front door. Gil 2 doesn't move.)* Go out and check if you want.
RAY 2. I want 'em back.
GIL 2. Sorry, they're my property.
RAY 2. *They're mine!* They were private, to you. They're who I am inside. They're not for other — Jesus, Gil.
GIL 2. Maybe I'll put 'em in the paper. Or hell — my travel editor might know somebody. "Gay Journal From The Heartland." What do you think?
RAY 2. It'll take away everything. I won't have them; I won't want you. Is that how you want it?
GIL 2. Is it worse than what I've got?
RAY 2. My whole life I've lived without you. I've been a farmer — we've lived different from each other.
GIL 2. You'll change.
RAY 2. I can't!
GIL 2. You change every day. You change in the time it takes to write a letter. You change whenever you dream, whenever you think about me. *(Ray 2 stares at Gil 2 a moment, then goes to the window and stares out.)*
RAY 2. Christ. Look where he's standing.
GIL 2. Who?
RAY 2. Your whatsisname, your ... Kit.
GIL 2. He's in the field.
RAY 2. Yeah — *where* in the field?
GIL 2. *Oh ...*
RAY 2. I've redug that thing three times. Deeper every time. Keep

41

dreaming about it.

GIL 2. Looks okay. I mean, nobody'd ever —

RAY 2. It just keeps sinking down, in my dream. Can't keep it level. Or dogs start digging there. Whole pack of dogs. Nightmare dogs. I wake up sweating. *(After a beat.)* What do you want? What do you want me to do?

GIL 2. I want us to take a week. You could come down to the Cities. You can tell Molly something, I'll tell Kit something. We can stay in a hotel and just … see.

RAY 2. I'm a farmer. I can't be gone a week.

GIL 2. Maybe not a whole week. Maybe a couple days. It might not take that long. We could realize right away that it's not going to work —

RAY 2. Can't tell you the last time I left this county. Even a couple days … No excuse would sound right to Molly.

GIL 2. If you don't find out now, when are you going to? Now's the time, Ray. Now's the chance. Don't let it all just … flow away again.

RAY 2. What do you think's going to happen in a few days in a hotel? *(After a beat.)* Is life even real to you, Gil? Do you care how many people you — ?

GIL 2. No. I don't care. Want to know why? 'Cause nobody up here ever once asked themselves, "What does Gil need? What's his deepest wish in life?"

RAY 2. They're not responsible for —

GIL 2. They were sitting in this town, all warm and toasty and accepted, while I was in the hospital, or down in the workhouse, or scraping my way through three abusive college relationships — all with guys that looked exactly like you —

RAY 2. We never —

GIL 2. *(Riding over.) Afraid to come home.* When did you ask me to come back, Ray? When did anybody? Not once. And you know what? Even if they had been asking, even if the whole town of Thief River had asked themselves what I needed, and if the answer had appeared on some huge marquee with eight billion lights: "GIL NEEDS RAY — GIL *REALLY* NEEDS RAY!" there'd be another whole question they never once in their lives wanted a serious answer to.

RAY 2. Which is?

42

GIL 2. "What does Ray need?" *(Ray 2 turns away from him.)* "What does Ray really need?" Why would they ask that question, when they could sleep through their whole lives, dreaming they knew you? *(After a beat.)* A few days. Together. Then you decide. I promise I won't bother you again.

RAY 2. No one sees the letters?

GIL 2. I didn't bring the letters.

RAY 2. What?

GIL 2. I didn't bring them, I was ... I was lying. I needed you to come.

RAY 2. Christ.

GIL 2. I had to think of a way. That's all. It was stupid.

RAY 2. That's an understatement. Where are my letters?

GIL 2. In my dresser, at home. I'll burn them if you want. We can burn them together. I'm sorry I held them over you. I would never have —

RAY 2. They're in your dresser? What — does Kit sit around reading them while you're at work?

GIL 2. He did read some. I should've known he'd look. He's so insecure. *(With a self-deprecating laugh.)* Not like me, right? *(Sighing.)* Anyhow, he started crying. And we had a long, long talk for about a ... century. He was literally sick with jealousy. For two weeks. Demanded that I break off all contact with you. I said I couldn't. Around then you stopped writing. He begged me to let it go at that. And I wanted to. I mean — he does love me ... as much as a twenty-one year-old can. He's gorgeous, ready to take care of me in my old age, and he's ... wrong. That's all; he's just wrong. *(After a beat.)* I'm sorry I lied to you. Why should you listen to me? I come up here to offer you something real and trustworthy, and ... I lie. I was never going to do that.

RAY 2. But you did.

GIL 2. *(After a beat.)* I'll burn the letters. *(Gil 2 turns for the front door.)*

RAY 2. You saved 'em all? Every one?

GIL 2. Yeah.

RAY 2. Twenty-five years?

GIL 2. I could tell you what it is in shoeboxes. *(After beat.)* Well. Tell Ray Junior I'm sorry. Tell him congratulations from me. *(A beat. Gil 2 starts out again.)*

RAY 2. I'll come down.

GIL 2. What?

RAY 2. Can only be a couple days —

GIL 2. That'd be all right.

RAY 2. You sure?

GIL 2. Whatever you can spare. Are you sure?

RAY 2. *(After a beat.)* Yeah.

GIL 2. I haven't had a dream like this in a long time.

RAY 2. Me neither. *(Suddenly the front door slams. Perry enters the room out of breath, alarmed.)*

PERRY. Ray! *Ray!!*

RAY 2. What!?

PERRY. Ray Junior's here! He just drove up!

RAY 2. *(Rushing to the window.)* Where?!

PERRY. Down by the tree — bottom of the driveway! He's got your friend!

GIL 2. Kit?! Oh, God ...

RAY 2. Oh, *God! (Ray 2 and Gil 2 rush out of the house. Perry stares out the window.)*

PERRY. He's beating the crap out of him. Damn tree — you can't see! But he's hurting him — bad! He could be killing him down there. *(Looking looks around, seeing they're gone.)* I'm coming! *(Perry hurries out. Lights shift as Gil 2 reenters and begins a "letter.")*

GIL 2. Dear Ray. I'm completely responsible. I don't know how many times I can say I'm sorry, but you deserve an apology that's ... infinite. Kit says he's sorry. I made Kit move out. Told him I could never trust him again. He cried ... for hours. He sits in his car now, outside my house. But I won't change my mind. Please write me again. Once. Please? I won't stop writing until you do. I mean it. I won't. I won't ever stop. *(Action continues as lights shift to:)*

# Scene 9

*2001. Ray 3 stares out the window. Gil 3 is sitting on his campstool. After a long moment, Ray 3 moves to his stool and sits with some difficulty.*

GIL 3. How long has that arm...?

RAY 3. Two years. Few months after Molly died.

GIL 3. I know you told me before. I just ...

RAY 3. You're old and you forget things.

GIL 3. Yeah. *(After a long beat.)* You're still handsome.

RAY 3. I know. *(They share a quiet laugh, which dies.)*

GIL 3. So Molly lived her whole life — ?

RAY 3. In the dark. That's right.

GIL 3. At least you think so.

RAY 3. It was dark enough; let me put it that way. *(After a beat.)* Whatever happened to Kit? You never said in your letters.

GIL 3. I don't like talking about Kit.

RAY 3. All right. Just wondered if he ever got himself to the "real" Brooklyn.

GIL 3. Yeah, he got himself to the "real" Brooklyn. And the real Village, and the real baths, and he got the real AIDS, and the real Kaposi's, and the real pneumocystis, and the real everything else — and he took the real three years to waste away and die.

RAY 3. I'm sorry.

GIL 3. Not that Brooklyn Center wouldn't've done. Plenty of people died there too. For a few years it felt like I was at Hennepin County Medical Center every damn day of my life. They should've given me my own parking spot.

RAY 3. I'm glad you didn't get sick.

GIL 3. Were you faithful to Molly? *(As Ray 3 gives him a long look.)* She's dead. No one'll know.

RAY 3. Yes. I was. Mostly. *(After a beat.)* Couple times I drove over to Grand Forks. You know, the air force base. There's places

... a few.

GIL 3. And?

RAY 3. Found a couple that looked like you. Never saw 'em again. That's a hundred forty miles, round trip. Pretty easy to give up on that.

GIL 3. I suppose.

RAY 3. All that just ... I don't know ... faded away. Plenty else to think about. You?

GIL 3. I don't know. After Kit left, after I made him go, it got tougher to ... get interested. Start avoiding getting involved. Didn't even notice it at first. Having a drink, having some talk ... started feeling like a good night.

RAY 3. Yeah.

GIL 3. Just the mechanical stuff, going to bed — not sure that was ever the main thing for me. It was important, but ... started to feel like I was doing more harm than good.

RAY 3. So you weren't ... with anybody?

GIL 3. I didn't feel so odd. And when HIV showed up, I started looking downright normal. For all I know, loving you saved my life.

RAY 3. God.

GIL 3. But don't think I didn't get sick. We all got sick. Whole community. I personally nursed four friends into the grave — people like me, that didn't have anyone. Or their lovers had bugged out, or died before them. There was one named Jim. He'd just finished building a log cabin on a lake when he got his diagnosis. And you know, he wanted to die up there, so ... I moved in and helped him die in his dream home. I got sick all right. Sick of waking up in that gorgeous place — that Eden — watching an invisible serpent devour my friend from the inside. Willed me the house. Had to sell it, couldn't live in it. *(A beat.)* So I guess we're lucky we never went to New York, you and me.

RAY 3. We'd've been all right; we'd've been faithful.

GIL 3. Long as there weren't any air force bases. *(They laugh despite themselves.)*

RAY 3. Who can ever know?

GIL 3. *(After a beat.)* Is Lewis still alive?

RAY 3. Yup.

GIL 3. God. They never die, do they?

RAY 3. Nope. He'll still fight anybody who says his hand got shot off by a fairy.

GIL 3. By a "fragile."

RAY 3. Claims he lost his fingers in the Korean War. Works with most people. *(They smile. A long beat.)*

GIL 3. I'm sorry you lost your wife.

RAY 3. Thank you. *(A beat.)* Lost the farm, too — don't forget that.

GIL 3. You must miss it.

RAY 3. Yeah. Town's not too bad.

GIL 3. I never liked it.

RAY 3. No, really. People are … people are fine. They don't pick sides that much.

GIL 3. Between you and your son?

RAY 3. They stay pretty neutral. *(After a beat.)* His mother never knew why he stopped talking to me. Gave her about ten different reasons over the years. She wouldn't let me give him the farm. Had to wait till she died.

GIL 3. I'm so sorry —

RAY 3. Don't even start. I don't want to hear it. I'd like to say I miss Ray Junior, but I really don't; that's the truth of it. *(With a quick look at him.)* Do miss having someone to talk to, though.

GIL 3. *(Not catching the hint.)* I imagine.

RAY 3. You must have a big circle of friends.

GIL 3. One or two, that's about it. They're still dying, you know. Different diseases, but they're still dying.

RAY 3. Yeah.

GIL 3. No cures for getting old yet.

RAY 3. *(After a beat.)* What if you stayed here?

GIL 3. What?

RAY 3. Move back. We could get a place together. *(A long silence. Gil 3 rises.)*

GIL 3. What are you saying?

RAY 3. Nothing. Just —

GIL 3. *Now* you want me to move in with you? Now?

RAY 3. Why not? We're both alone —

GIL 3. I've been alone for almost thirty years. It's not like an emergency for me, Ray.

RAY 3. I didn't mean that.

GIL 3. My life works very well the way it is.

RAY 3. I'm sure it does —

GIL 3. It's not like I didn't wait for you — right? I did wait for you.

RAY 3. I know that.

GIL 3. Pretty much my whole life. I mean, that would be a fair estimate?

RAY 3. Pretty much.

GIL 3. And never once in that time did you give me the slightest — *(Stopping himself.)* But now, now Molly is dead, *now* you think I should drop everything and everyone else in my life and just move in with you?

RAY 3. It's just that we're alone —

GIL 3. Get a nurse! I've done my share — more than my share — of that crap! I don't need to help one more hopeless … *wreck* find his way to eternity. Okay? I don't need that.

RAY 3. *(After a beat.)* Of course not. Sorry I —

GIL 3. And if you think I'm going to have someone like you looking after me — I mean, if I go dotty first — then you are seriously deluded.

RAY 3. It was a bad —

GIL 3. No it wasn't bad, Ray. It wasn't bad, it was unloving. *(After a beat.)* You didn't say, "Gil, I still love you. I always have, but I was a coward. I was afraid to act on my love. I preferred a life of lying to everyone around me. I was a fool, and so I got half a life, and I sentenced you to the same." You didn't say that. You just said, "Well, we're both alone."

RAY 3. Gil —

GIL 3. We're born alone, Ray. We die alone. And every minute of our lives is a chance not to be alone anymore. But it takes a lot. It's not just a matter of being with somebody. Not just touching them, seeing them every morning.

RAY 3. I know.

GIL 3. I'm sure you do. I know you do. You wrote me. *(After a beat.)* You haven't heard from me in ten years. There's a reason, Ray. Not even I can wait forever. *(Jody runs in the front door, stopping at the archway. He's out of breath.)*

JODY. That Reese guy wants you to come out. Says the court order —

RAY 3. Tell him we can't —

GIL 3. No. It's fine. I'll go out.

RAY 3. You'll just get in a fight with him.

GIL 3. No, I won't. Don't feel angry anymore. Finally got mad at the right person. *(Gil 3 circles out of the room, past Jody.)*

JODY. He okay?

RAY 3. Sure.

JODY. You?

RAY 3. Now when'd you ever care how I was feeling?

JODY. Who said I cared? *(As they share a smile.)* What was he yelling about? I could hear him outside.

RAY 3. This and that. Lifetime of things. You know how it is.

JODY. Yeah, I know how it is. *(They smile again. A beat.)*

RAY 3. Do you love me?

JODY. What?

RAY 3. Not like your Grandpa. Not even like someone you grew up with. Like a person. Some people you love, some you don't. So — knowing all I am — knowing what I am, do you love me?

JODY. Yeah.

RAY 3. I love you, too.

JODY. *(After a beat.)* That was weird. *(They freeze. Lights shift as Gil 3 enters. They move off, directly across the floor, as Gil 3 addresses the audience.)*

GIL 3. For years I wrote travel books. Articles, features for the paper. Never left the region, though. Upper Midwest, central Canada — that's all I did. Told everyone I was afraid to fly. I sometimes imagined if you drew a circle around all the places I wrote up, the center of that circle would be ... Well. You know what it would be. *(Gil 3 exits as lights shift to:)*

# Scene 10

*1973. Gil 2 tends to Kit, who's been badly beaten. Ray 2, who looks as though he's been in a struggle, stands looking on.*

KIT. Ow! Stop it! That hurts.

GIL 2. You have to tell me what hurts —

KIT. It all hurts! It all does! *Christ!*

RAY 2. Think anything's broken?

GIL 2. I don't know. Doesn't seem like it.

KIT. How do you know? You're not a doctor.

RAY 2. You want to see a doctor?

KIT. No! Not till I'm back in the city! I don't want anybody out here to touch me!

PERRY. *(Entering, going to the window.)* He's going now. Nope — there's his brake lights again. It's like he can't decide.

GIL 2. Why'd he hit you, Kit? Why'd he beat you up?

KIT. I don't know …

PERRY. Kit was just sitting on his car. I was over by the creek. Can't believe Ray Junior kept going at him like that. *(Looking out the window.)* His brake lights are still on. He's just hanging there.

KIT. Don't be mad at me, Gil. Please don't be mad.

GIL 2. Why should I be mad? What happened?

KIT. Nothing. I didn't do anything! Just … the letter.

RAY 2. What?

GIL 2. Kit — what letter?

RAY 2. What letter?!

KIT It wasn't my fault! He grabbed me! He started hitting me! I showed him a letter — you know, from his Dad.

RAY 2. Gil —

GIL 2. There aren't any letters! I didn't bring them!

KIT. I took one.

GIL 2. *What?!*

RAY 2. Perry, get out of here.

KIT. *(To Perry.)* He's got a whole dresser full of letters. Think he's got any from me?

GIL 2. We live together. We don't write letters.

KIT. There was that postcard! *(To Perry.)* I went to the Black Hills.

RAY 2. Gil —

PERRY. What letter?

RAY 2. *(To Perry.)* Will you just get out of here!?

PERRY. What letter!?

KIT. I took one of 'em.

GIL 2. *Why?*

KIT. 'Cause I wanted to! 'Cause the world's full of Ray Juniors! *(A beat.)* He was beating on me — I could barely get the damn thing out. I said, "Here — your Dad wrote this! Check the handwriting." And he just kept on hitting me! I stuffed it in his pocket —

GIL 2. Oh, God — *(Ray 2 goes to the window. He stares out.)*

RAY 2. He's got it now?

KIT. Yeah.

PERRY. His brake lights are still on. He's probably reading it. That's why he ain't going. *(To Ray 2.)* What does it say? What does it say?

KIT. I memorized it. It says, "Gil, I was down at the place where the river hooks around that rock, where it gets lazy in the sun and the fish swim in circles over warm sand. I stood there a long time, remembering how you laid on that rock — "

GIL 2. *(Quietly.)* Stop it.

KIT. "How my hand went over your shoulders and down your beautiful, slim back, and over — "

GIL 2. *(As before.)* Stop it.

KIT. "And down between your legs and found you there — hard, warm like the rock. Our last time there. We didn't know it. We laid there the whole day, staring at the sky."

GIL 2. Oh, God.

PERRY. Jesus.

RAY 2. He's reading that. Right now. Sitting in his car, staring at the fields. His foot's on the brake, and he's reading that.

PERRY. Jesus. Does Molly know?

RAY 2. No.

PERRY. Jesus.

GIL 2. *(To Kit.)* Why'd you do it? *Why'd you do it!!?*

KIT. Why do you think? I love you!

GIL 2. Christ.

KIT. 'Course you don't care; I'm not Ray. You barely know I'm around. Just something to hug 'cause Ray's not there.

GIL 2. Kit —

KIT. I love you! You treat me like shit, and I love you. *(Kit starts to cry softly in his arms.)*

PERRY. No one's telling Molly. No one's telling her. If Ray Junior tries to tell her — *(Looking out the window.)* He's going! *(Starting for the door.)* I gotta stop him! Ray — !

RAY 2. Take my car. Keys are in it. *(As Perry hurries out, looking out the window.)* "We laid there the whole day, staring at the sky."

GIL 2. Ray —

RAY 2. The sky just fell, Gil.

GIL 2. No …

RAY 2. It just fell. *(Ray 2 walks out without looking back.)*

GIL 2. *(Trying to get up.)* Ray! Ray — !!

KIT. Don't go —

GIL 2. *Ray — !!*

KIT. *(Clutching at him.)* Don't go — !! *(They freeze. Lights shift as Gil 2 and Kit rise and exit slowly. Spotlight on Gil 3 as he begins a "letter.")*

GIL 3. Dear Ray. This must be how you felt when you wrote me for the last time. Guess I don't feel as angry. Feel as empty, though. Maybe you won't even read this. You probably rip my letters up without reading them. Twenty years' worth. Think I said I'm sorry every possible way there is. If there's one I've missed, don't bother to tell me. Goodbye. Gil. *(Gil 3 exits. Action continues as lights shift to.)*

# Scene 11

*1948. Gil sits unmoving on the floor, near the window. After a few moments, Anson enters, followed by Ray. Their clothes are dirty; they've been digging. Anson carries the gun in his belt. Ray sits tiredly, across the room from Gil. Anson stands looking at the two of them.*

ANSON. Ray and me have been digging out back.
GIL. How could you — ?
ANSON. We were burying a stray dog I killed. Looked kinda funny, like it might have rabies. Suppose we should've reported it to the county health officer, but we didn't. Just shot it and buried it, like they did a hundred years ago. Shot it and buried it and forgot all about it. That dog might've bit you — both of you. You'd've died.
GIL. How could you let him — ?
RAY. I didn't know what he was gonna do! I thought he was gonna just scare him.
ANSON. You never take a chance on a rabid dog.
GIL. He was a man.
ANSON. So he could talk. *(Pulling Harlow's razor from his pocket.)* A dog that could talk. He ain't gonna talk anymore. Ain't gonna bite anybody, either. I saved your lives. Most folks'd say thank you. *(A silence.)*
GIL. What'll we tell the police?
ANSON. You don't go to the police when you bury a dog. It's forgotten.
GIL. But —
RAY. Gil, he's right. It's done. We did it. We have to keep it a secret now.
ANSON. If we don't, we all go to prison.
RAY. You want to go to prison for somebody like that?
GIL. I'll still have to talk to the police. I shot Lewis, remember?
ANSON. The kid at the dance? *(Gil stares at Anson.)*
RAY. I told him.

ANSON. You've had a busy night.

GIL. So have you.

ANSON. Don't smart-mouth me. If you ever mention Harlow I'll kill you myself, 'cause I'll have nothing to lose. Is that understood?

GIL. Yes, sir.

ANSON. I should kill you now for touching my grandson. Bury you beside that other dog. *(After a silence.)* You talk to the police about this Lewis boy, and you take your medicine. They'll probably give you time in the workhouse or send you to the army. Either way, you'll be gone. When you get out, don't come back.

GIL. What?

RAY. Grandpa —

ANSON. Don't ever show up in Thief River again. Is that clear?

RAY. You can't —

ANSON. *Quiet!! (To Gil.)* I'm gonna give you two options, son. You're gonna take one. It's an ultimatum. You understand what that word means?

GIL. Yes, sir.

ANSON. You understand it's final.

GIL. Yes.

ANSON. People don't understand what final means. Harlow understands.

GIL. Yes, sir.

ANSON. When you leave this town, and you will, don't come back. Ever. Don't talk about Harlow, and especially don't talk about anything you did to my grandson. That's your first choice. I think it's your best one.

GIL. What if I do come back?

ANSON. I'll kill you.

GIL. Just for — ?

RAY. You can't —

ANSON. If you live here, people will know. They will know you for what you are. Hell, I suppose they already do, some of 'em. What went on between you and Ray'll get out, in time. It'll ruin his life. I won't let that happen.

GIL. I'll just come back and tell everybody right out.

RAY. *(Alarmed.)* Gil — !

ANSON. *(Moving close to Gil.)* I almost hope you do that. 'Cause

54

then when I kill you, I can get off. They won't convict me. I'll just tell 'em you slandered my grandson and tried to ruin my family name. 'Round here, they'll probably elect me mayor. But let's say you do come back and blab it all around, and let's say I kill you. Where's that gonna leave Ray? If you really love Ray ... do you love him?

GIL. Yes.

ANSON. Then you'll want to see his life work out. Ray's had enough tragedy. He needs the farm, needs a wife, needs children. Needs respect. Needs people believing in him. None of that'll happen if you talk. And if you're here, I think you will talk, eventually. You don't look like a kid who keeps secrets too well.

GIL. I don't.

RAY. Gil.

GIL. It's true though. I don't. Half the kids at school know what I'm like. Maybe they all do. I can't hide it. I don't know how.

ANSON. *(Playing with the razor.)* So that's it. Either leave and stay gone, or come back and I'll kill you. Which'll it be?

GIL. Ray? We could move away.

RAY. Move away?

GIL. Just leave! Both of us! Together.

ANSON. And go where?

RAY. I live here. This is my house. This was ... gonna be my house. I live here.

GIL. But if we don't, we can't ... we can't ... *Ray* — !

RAY. This is my farm —

GIL. *Get another one!*

RAY. How? I couldn't do that. Where would I get the money?

GIL. What are you saying? Are you saying — what are you saying to me?

RAY. Maybe he's right. Maybe it's not safe for you here. Not safe for anybody.

GIL. You're telling me to go?

RAY. It's your only choice.

GIL. It's no choice! How can that be a choice!? You know what it's been like since you stopped seeing me!?

RAY. I can't help that —

GIL. Of course you can —

RAY. *I have to have my life!* Gil? I have to have my life. *(A beat.)*

55

GIL. Go ahead then. Go ahead. *(Gil suddenly rushes at a startled Anson and grabs the closed razor from his hand.)*
ANSON. Hey — ! *(Gil retreats again and opens the razor. Gil stares directly at Ray as he draws it down in a quick stroke, slashing his own neck from just below his ear to near his collar bone. Ray screams and rushes to him. Anson grabs Ray.)*
RAY. *NO — !! Gil, don't — !!*
ANSON. Let him! *(Ray rushes to Gil, who's bleeding. The blood isn't spurting, though. He's missed the major vessels. Ray grabs the razor, pulls out a handkerchief and presses it to the wound as best he can. Gil is near fainting — more from the shock of what he's done than from the wound itself.)*
RAY. You'll be all right. You'll be all right! Gil! Gil, stay with me!
ANSON. Let him die.
RAY. *He's not gonna die!* We're taking him to the hospital!
ANSON. Ray —
RAY. We're taking him! Start the car! *(Anson exits.)* Come on, Gil. Stay awake. We'll get you fixed up.
GIL. *(Groggily.)* I'm sorry …
RAY. We'll fix you. Make you like new. Nothing will be wrong with you. Nothing will be wrong with you anymore.
GIL. I'm sorry, Ray
RAY. It's all right.
GIL. I'm sorry.
RAY. You're gonna be all right. You're gonna be perfect. *(They freeze as lights shift to:)*


# Scene 12


*2001. Ray 3 enters past the motionless Ray and Gil and stands looking out the window. After a moment, Gil 3 enters.*


GIL 3. What happened to the stools?
RAY 3. Jody put 'em in the car. Time to leave?

56

GIL 3. *(Nodding.)* Harlow has … disappeared. Dust sitting on a lot of other dust. Good feeling. Maybe you were right.

RAY 3. Don't go overboard.

GIL 3. Makes you wonder, though.

RAY 3. About what?

GIL 3. Who might be hitting you in the face when the wind blows.

RAY 3. *(Moving toward the door.)* And on that cheery note —

GIL 3. Thank you.

RAY 3. For what?

GIL 3. For inviting me.

RAY 3. *(After a beat.)* You're welcome.

GIL 3. I'd gotten so used to you not being … possible.

RAY 3. I understand.

GIL 3. What if that's the whole attraction? *(Ray 3 nods thoughtfully. Gil 3 starts to to move slowly toward the front door.)*

RAY 3. I'd hate to think about this house being torn down without you here to see it.

GIL 3. Yeah. Maybe I'll come up for a visit.

RAY 3. You could stay with me. Place is small, but there'd be room.

GIL 3. *(Stopping.)* People might talk.

RAY 3. If we're lucky. You remember that trail through Culley's field? Where the grass is so tall? We used to hide in there and —

GIL 3. I remember.

RAY 3. Jody and I went by there the other day. It looks just the same. *(Ray 3 exits. Gil 3 starts to follow him, then pauses and takes a last look around the room. He focuses on the tableau of the two boys for a moment, then exits. Lights slowly fade on Ray and Gil.)*

## End of Play

# PROPERTY LIST

Three nylon fold-out camp stools
Bottle of tonic water with top broken off (RAY)
Straight razor (HARLOW, GIL, ANSON)
Funeral urn containing ashes (JODY, GIL)
Gun (RAY, ANSON)
Keys (RAY, GIL)
Belt (RAY)
Wallet (HARLOW, GIL)
Shovel (ANSON)
Handkerchief (RAY)

# SOUND EFFECTS

Sound of sparrows in tree
A storm of beating wings
Door being forced open
Screen door slams
Muffled smash of glass
Floor squeaks
Floor creaks four times
Front door slams
Sound of someone running off
Gunshot

# NEW PLAYS

★ **THE CREDEAUX CANVAS by Keith Bunin.** A forged painting leads to tragedy among friends. "There is that moment between adolescence and middle age when being disaffected looks attractive. Witness the enduring appeal of Prince Hamlet, Jake Barnes and James Dean, on the stage, page and screen. Or, more immediately, take a look at the lithe young things in THE CREDEAUX CANVAS..." –*NY Times.* "THE CREDEAUX CANVAS is the third recent play about painters...it turned out to be the best of the lot, better even than most plays about non-painters." –*NY Magazine.* [2M, 2W] ISBN: 0-8222-1838-0

★ **THE DIARY OF ANNE FRANK by Frances Goodrich and Albert Hackett, newly adapted by Wendy Kesselman.** A transcendently powerful new adaptation in which Anne Frank emerges from history a living, lyrical, intensely gifted young girl. "Undeniably moving. It shatters the heart. The evening never lets us forget the inhuman darkness waiting to claim its incandescently human heroine." –*NY Times.* "A sensitive, stirring and thoroughly engaging new adaptation." –*NY Newsday.* "A powerful new version that moves the audience to gasps, then tears." –*A.P.* "One of the year's ten best." –*Time Magazine.* [5M, 5W, 3 extras] ISBN: 0-8222-1718-X

★ **THE BOOK OF LIZ by David Sedaris and Amy Sedaris.** Sister Elizabeth Donderstock makes the cheese balls that support her religious community, but feeling unappreciated among the Squeamish, she decides to try her luck in the outside world. "...[a] delightfully off-key, off-color hymn to clichés we all live by, whether we know it or not." –*NY Times.* "Good-natured, goofy and frequently hilarious..." –*NY Newsday.* "...[THE BOOK OF LIZ] may well be the world's first Amish picaresque...hilarious..." –*Village Voice.* [2M, 2W (doubling, flexible casting to 8M, 7W)] ISBN: 0-8222-1827-5

★ **JAR THE FLOOR by Cheryl L. West.** A quartet of black women spanning four generations makes up this hilarious and heartwarming dramatic comedy. "...a moving and hilarious account of a black family sparring in a Chicago suburb..." –*NY Magazine.* "...heart-to-heart confrontations and surprising revelations...first-rate..." –*NY Daily News.* "...unpretentious good feelings...bubble through West's loving and humorous play..." –*Star-Ledger.* "...one of the wisest plays I've seen in ages...[from] a master playwright." –*USA Today.* [5W] ISBN: 0-8222-1809-7

★ **THIEF RIVER by Lee Blessing.** Love between two men over decades is explored in this incisive portrait of coming to terms with who you are. "Mr. Blessing unspools the plot ingeniously, skipping back and forth in time as the details require...an absorbing evening." –*NY Times.* "...wistful and sweet-spirited..." –*Variety.* [6M] ISBN: 0-8222-1839-9

★ **THE BEGINNING OF AUGUST by Tom Donaghy.** When Jackie's wife abruptly and mysteriously leaves him and their infant daughter, a pungently comic reevaluation of suburban life ensues. "Donaghy holds a cracked mirror up to the contemporary American family, anatomizing its frailties and miscommunications in fractured language that can be both funny and poignant." –*The Philadelphia Inquirer.* "...[A] sharp, eccentric new comedy. Pungently funny...fresh and precise..." –*LA Times.* [3M, 2W] ISBN: 0-8222-1786-4

★ **OUTSTANDING MEN'S MONOLOGUES 2001–2002 and OUTSTANDING WOMEN'S MONOLOGUES 2001–2002 edited by Craig Pospisil.** Drawn exclusively from Dramatists Play Service publications, these collections for actors feature over fifty monologues each and include an enormous range of voices, subject matter and characters. MEN'S ISBN: 0-8222-1821-6 WOMEN'S ISBN: 0-8222-1822-4

**DRAMATISTS PLAY SERVICE, INC.**
440 Park Avenue South, New York, NY 10016 212-683-8960 Fax 212-213-1539
postmaster@dramatists.com www.dramatists.com

# NEW PLAYS

★ **A LESSON BEFORE DYING by Romulus Linney, based on the novel by Ernest J. Gaines.** An innocent young man is condemned to death in backwoods Louisiana and must learn to die with dignity. "The story's wrenching power lies not in its outrage but in the almost inexplicable grace the characters must muster as their only resistance to being treated like lesser beings." *–The New Yorker.* "Irresistable momentum and a cathartic explosion…a powerful inevitability." *–NY Times.* [5M, 2W] ISBN: 0-8222-1785-6

★ **BOOM TOWN by Jeff Daniels.** A searing drama mixing small-town love, politics and the consequences of betrayal. "…a brutally honest, contemporary foray into classic themes, exploring what moves people to lie, cheat, love and dream. By BOOM TOWN's climactic end there are no secrets, only bare truth." *–Oakland Press.* "…some of the most electrifying writing Daniels has ever done…" *–Ann Arbor News.* [2M, 1W] ISBN: 0-8222-1760-0

★ **INCORRUPTIBLE by Michael Hollinger.** When a motley order of medieval monks learns their patron saint no longer works miracles, a larcenous, one-eyed minstrel shows them an outrageous new way to pay old debts. "A lightning-fast farce, rich in both verbal and physical humor." *–American Theatre.* "Everything fits snugly in this funny, endearing black comedy…an artful blend of the mock-formal and the anachronistically breezy…A piece of remarkably dexterous craftsmanship." *–Philadelphia Inquirer.* "A farcical romp, scintillating and irreverent." *–Philadelphia Weekly.* [5M, 3W] ISBN: 0-8222-1787-2

★ **CELLINI by John Patrick Shanley.** Chronicles the life of the original "Renaissance Man," Benvenuto Cellini, the sixteenth-century Italian sculptor and man-about-town. Adapted from the autobiography of Benvenuto Cellini, translated by J. Addington Symonds. "[Shanley] has created a convincing Cellini, not neglecting his dark side, and a trim, vigorous, fast-moving show." *–BackStage.* "Very entertaining…With brave purpose, the narrative undermines chronology before untangling it…touching and funny…" *–NY Times.* [7M, 2W (doubling)] ISBN: 0-8222-1808-9

★ **PRAYING FOR RAIN by Robert Vaughan.** Examines a burst of fatal violence and its aftermath in a suburban high school. "Thought provoking and compelling." *–Denver Post.* "Vaughan's powerful drama offers hope and possibilities." *–Theatre.com.* "[The play] doesn't put forth compact, tidy answers to the problem of youth violence. What it does offer is a compelling exploration of the forces that influence an individual's choices, and of the proverbial lifelines—be they familial, communal, religious or political—that tragically slacken when society gives in to apathy, fear and self-doubt…" *–Westword.* "…a symphony of anger…" *–Gazette Telegraph.* [4M, 3W] ISBN: 0-8222-1807-0

★ **GOD'S MAN IN TEXAS by David Rambo.** When a young pastor takes over one of the most prestigious Baptist churches from a rip-roaring old preacher-entrepreneur, all hell breaks loose. "…the pick of the litter of all the works at the Humana Festival…" *–Providence Journal.* "…a wealth of both drama and comedy in the struggle for power…" *–LA Times.* "…the first act is so funny…deepens in the second act into a sobering portrait of fear, hope and self-delusion…" *–Columbus Dispatch.* [3M] ISBN: 0-8222-1801-1

★ **JESUS HOPPED THE 'A' TRAIN by Stephen Adly Guirgis.** A probing, intense portrait of lives behind bars at Rikers Island. "…fire-breathing…whenever it appears that JESUS is settling into familiar territory, it slides right beneath expectations into another, fresher direction. It has the courage of its intellectual restlessness…[JESUS HOPPED THE 'A' TRAIN] has been written in flame." *–NY Times.* [4M, 1W] ISBN: 0-8222-1799-6

**DRAMATISTS PLAY SERVICE, INC.**
440 Park Avenue South, New York, NY 10016  212-683-8960  Fax 212-213-1539
postmaster@dramatists.com  www.dramatists.com

# NEW PLAYS

★ **THE CIDER HOUSE RULES, PARTS 1 & 2 by Peter Parnell, adapted from the novel by John Irving.** Spanning eight decades of American life, this adaptation from the Irving novel tells the story of Dr. Wilbur Larch, founder of the St. Cloud's, Maine orphanage and hospital, and of the complex father-son relationship he develops with the young orphan Homer Wells. "...luxurious digressions, confident pacing...an enterprise of scope and vigor..." –*NY Times.* "...The fact that I can't wait to see Part 2 only begins to suggest just how good it is..." –*NY Daily News.* "...engrossing...an odyssey that has only one major shortcoming: It comes to an end." –*Seattle Times.* "...outstanding...captures the humor, the humility...of Irving's 588-page novel..." –*Seattle Post-Intelligencer.* [9M, 10W, doubling, flexible casting] PART 1 ISBN: 0-8222-1725-2 PART 2 ISBN: 0-8222-1726-0

★ **TEN UNKNOWNS by Jon Robin Baitz.** An iconoclastic American painter in his seventies has his life turned upside down by an art dealer and his ex-boyfriend. "...breadth and complexity...a sweet and delicate harmony rises from the four cast members...Mr. Baitz is without peer among his contemporaries in creating dialogue that spontaneously conveys a character's social context and moral limitations..." –*NY Times.* "...darkly funny, brilliantly desperate comedy...TEN UNKNOWNS vibrates with vital voices." –*NY Post.* [3M, 1W] ISBN: 0-8222-1826-7

★ **BOOK OF DAYS by Lanford Wilson.** A small-town actress playing St. Joan struggles to expose a murder. "...[Wilson's] best work since *Fifth of July*...An intriguing, prismatic and thoroughly engrossing depiction of contemporary small-town life with a murder mystery at its core...a splendid evening of theater..." –*Variety.* "...fascinating...a densely populated, unpredictable little world." –*St. Louis Post-Dispatch.* [6M, 5W] ISBN: 0-8222-1767-8

★ **THE SYRINGA TREE by Pamela Gien.** Winner of the 2001 Obie Award. A breathtakingly beautiful tale of growing up white in apartheid South Africa. "Instantly engaging, exotic, complex, deeply shocking...a thoroughly persuasive transport to a time and a place...stun[s] with the power of a gut punch..." –*NY Times.* "Astonishing...affecting ...[with] a dramatic and heartbreaking conclusion...A deceptive sweet simplicity haunts THE SYRINGA TREE..." –*A.P.* [1W (or flexible cast)] ISBN: 0-8222-1792-9

★ **COYOTE ON A FENCE by Bruce Graham.** An emotionally riveting look at capital punishment. "The language is as precise as it is profane, provoking both troubling thought and the occasional cheerful laugh...will change you a little before it lets go of you." –*Cincinnati CityBeat.* "...excellent theater in every way..." –*Philadelphia City Paper.* [3M, 1W] ISBN: 0-8222-1738-4

★ **THE PLAY ABOUT THE BABY by Edward Albee.** Concerns a young couple who have just had a baby and the strange turn of events that transpire when they are visited by an older man and woman. "An invaluable self-portrait of sorts from one of the few genuinely great living American dramatists...rockets into that special corner of theater heaven where words shoot off like fireworks into dazzling patterns and hues." –*NY Times.* "An exhilarating, wicked...emotional terrorism." –*NY Newsday.* [2M, 2W] ISBN: 0-8222-1814-3

★ **FORCE CONTINUUM by Kia Corthron.** Tensions among black and white police officers and the neighborhoods they serve form the backdrop of this discomfiting look at life in the inner city. "The creator of this intense...new play is a singular voice among American playwrights...exceptionally eloquent..." –*NY Times.* "...a rich subject and a wise attitude." –*NY Post.* [6M, 2W, 1 boy] ISBN: 0-8222-1817-8

**DRAMATISTS PLAY SERVICE, INC.**
440 Park Avenue South, New York, NY 10016  212-683-8960  Fax 212-213-1539
postmaster@dramatists.com  www.dramatists.com